"This is an excellent book that brings together a faith-based approach and brain science. Charles Thompson offers proven strategies to help suffering people find some relief."

John Arden, PhD, ABPP
Author of Brain Based Therapy for OCD:
A Workbook for Clinicians and Clients

"In *Jesus and OCD*, Pastor Charles Thompson encourages, challenges, and inspires believers in Christ to face obsessive-compulsive disorder head-on by transparently sharing his own struggles with this illness and the strategies that have helped him fight it."

Peter A. Johnson, M.D.
White Stone Building
26205 Oak Ridge Dr.
Spring, TX 77380

Charles Thompson, a person who gives everything of himself to serve Jesus by serving others, pours into everything he does an extreme amount of care. Knowing his steadfast Christian character and desire for doing everything very well, he has no doubt put together a valuable resource for Christians struggling with this issue. Several years ago he shared with me a bit about his struggles with OCD. Just speaking with him helped me understand needs and struggles a person with OCD faces. He also helped me understand that although he faces these struggles daily, he has found ways of dealing with this from a specifically Christian perspective. May the reader of this workbook be blessed with the reassurance that they are not alone, indeed many godly people struggle here. And may they know that there is hope!

Angela Zgarba
Homeschooling Mother of Two
Former Public School Educator
Former Children's Ministry Director
London, KY 40741

"I thank the Lord for the wisdom that He gave Pastor Charles Thompson to be able to encourage in a powerful way the fight against OCD. He shares from his heart how he struggles with this illness and how the Spirit of God can give power, love, and self-discipline. You can find a way out not only from OCD, but other fears you may have."

Carolina Hornor
Loving with Mercy Ministries
Missionary to El Salvador
Kerman, California 93630

This workbook spiritually maps out a way for Christians who struggle with OCD, to find a path of freedom while navigating life's journey. It speaks honestly and raw about the daily mental struggle and then gives specific application on how to see oneself from God's perspective. It is a very thoughtful read!

Jami-Jon Pearson, Ph.D.
Raleigh, NC

"I am so thankful for my friend, Charles. We used to play GI JOE together as boys, and now we are co-laborers for Christ and His kingdom. I count it a joy and privilege to partner with him as he is a man of character and integrity, with a deep love for Christ and His church. Charles is on the front lines of this spiritual battle. He understands the pain, fears, and reality of the battle. In his book, not only will you be encouraged if you struggle with OCD, but you will get practical helps from someone who has been, and is on the journey with you. The Jesus and OCD workbook is practical, authentic, and Biblical. I will keep this in my library as a valuable and rich resource!"

John Sherrill
Lead Pastor, Declaration Church
Spring TX

I met and became friends with Charles Thompson over fifteen years ago. He has always been a solid pastor who effectively helps others. In Jesus and OCD, he has carefully designed a workbook that will help people struggling with OCD. His workbook couples the encouragement and power of the scripture with effective methods to alleviate what some feel unbearable. Pastor Thompson speaks from his own experience, by willingly sharing his own struggles and victories while offering others the opportunity to overcome OCD step by step. Don't overlook this workbook and the opportunity to experience the path of healing in your life.

Mike Swendson. MA., Pastor, College Educator
Holton, KS 66436

JESUS
AND
OCD

A Christian Workbook for Overcoming
Obsessive Compulsive Disorder

Charles Thompson

WESTBOW
PRESS®
A DIVISION OF THOMAS NELSON
& ZONDERVAN

All Scripture quotations, unless otherwise indicated, are taken from the Holy Bible, New International Version®, NIV®. Copyright ©1973, 1978, 1984, 2011 by Biblica, Inc.™ Used by permission of Zondervan. All rights reserved worldwide. www.zondervan.com The "NIV" and "New International Version" are trademarks registered in the United States Patent and Trademark Office by Biblica, Inc.™

Scripture taken from the New Century Version®. Copyright © 2005 by Thomas Nelson. Used by permission. All rights reserved.

Scripture quotations taken from the Amplified® Bible (AMP), Copyright © 2015 by The Lockman Foundation Used by permission. www.Lockman.org.

Scripture quotations are taken from the Holy Bible, New Living Translation, copyright ©1996, 2004, 2007, 2013, 2015 by Tyndale House Foundation. Used by permission of Tyndale House Publishers, Inc., Carol Stream, Illinois 60188. All rights reserved.

Scripture quotations marked (KJV) are from the King James Version.

Excerpts from BRAIN LOCK by JEFFREY M. SCHWARTZ, M.D..COPYRIGHT © 1996 BY JEFFREY M. SCHWARTZ, M.D. Reprinted by permission of HarperCollins Publishers.

WestBow Press books may be ordered through booksellers or by contacting:

WestBow Press
A Division of Thomas Nelson & Zondervan
1663 Liberty Drive
Bloomington, IN 47403
www.westbowpress.com
844-714-3454

ISBN: 978-1-5127-8379-7 (sc)
ISBN: 978-1-5127-8380-3 (hc)
ISBN: 978-1-5127-8378-0 (e)

Library of Congress Control Number: 2017906136

Print information available on the last page.

WestBow Press rev. date: 07/29/2017

This book is dedicated to all the Christians in this world who have Obsessive Compulsive Disorder and are looking for hope. Hope is a person and His name is Jesus!

I would also like to thank everyone who made this project possible by giving a donation to cover my part of the publishing process. You made a difference in my life and by your support will make a difference for others with OCD. Praise God!

CONTENTS

CHAPTER 1

Why This Book?

I WISH THAT I could tell you that there are no Christians who suffer with what is known as obsessive compulsive disorder. The fact is that there are many who do struggle with it, and I am one of those who have had to learn how to live with the disorder.

I have called out to the Lord on numerous occasions for obsessive compulsive disorder to be removed from my body. As of the writing of this workbook, I have to recite the words of the Apostle Paul.

Three times I pleaded with the Lord to take it away from me. But he said to me, "My grace is sufficient for you, for my power is made perfect in weakness." Therefore I will boast all the more gladly about my weaknesses, so that Christ's power may rest on me. That is why, for Christ's sake, I delight in weaknesses, in insults, in hardships, in persecutions, in difficulties. For when I am weak, then I am strong. (2 Corinthians 12:8-10).

I have found that God's grace is sufficient for what I have faced and that He has also made me strong in the weakness of this disorder.

I know with all of my heart, no matter how hopeless you feel, He will do the same for you. There are also some additional words of Paul that lead me to write this workbook.

Praise be to the God and Father of our Lord Jesus Christ, the Father of compassion and the God of all comfort, who comforts us in all our troubles, so that we can comfort those in any trouble with the comfort we ourselves receive from God. 2 Corinthians 1:3-4

The same help that God has given me through my journey with OCD was not meant to stop with me. The comfort that He gave me is meant to be extended to others who suffer. Why? I am able to identify with someone else who has the disorder unlike someone who does not have it. I have shared with others through the years my battle with OCD hoping to find some help, where many times I was met with a lack of understanding since they could not comprehend what I was going through. You will not get that from me in this workbook. I walk in your shoes. I also absolutely refuse to let what I have been through be a waste. If I hide it in shame, then it is wasted. God wastes no hurt! He wants to redeem it by using it to minister to others.

On my journey, I also found that there were no Christian workbooks to assist believers with obsessive compulsive disorder. Thus, I felt compelled to provide one as God has something to say about the condition. It is not something to be treated only by the medical community. As this short chapter is wrapped up, it is appropriate to make sure that you are a believer. A relationship with God will allow the best benefit from this course.

You are a *sinner.*

For all have sinned and fall short of the glory of God. Romans 3:23

You need a *Savior.*

For God so loved the world that he gave his one and only Son, that whoever believes in him shall not perish but have eternal life. For God did not send his Son into the world to condemn the world, but to save the world through him. Whoever believes in him is not condemned, but whoever does not believe stands condemned already because they have not believed in the name of God's one and only Son. John 3:16-17

You need to *call* on Him.

But what does it say? "The word is near you; it is in your mouth and in your heart," that is, the message concerning faith that we proclaim: If you declare with your mouth, "Jesus is Lord," and believe in your heart that God raised him from the dead, you will be saved. For it is with your heart that you believe and are justified, and it is with your mouth that you profess your faith and are saved. As Scripture says, "Anyone who believes in him will never be put to shame." Romans 10:8-11

Are you ready to start a personal relationship with God? Pray the following...

Jesus, I invite you to come into my life. I am a sinner and need someone to save me from my sins that separate me from You. Thank you for dying on the cross for me, and I ask for the forgiveness that You offer. I rejoice that I am getting a new start, in which my sins are thrown to the bottom of the sea to be remembered no more, and are removed from me as far as east is from the west.

Now, let us move back to some introduction questions to consider.

1. *How do you think God's grace can help you with obsessive compulsive disorder?*

2. *How do you think God's strength can help you with obsessive compulsive disorder?*

3. *How do you think you can use what you have been through with obsessive compulsive disorder to identify with and help others?*

CHAPTER 2

I Choose Joshua and Caleb

Y OU MUST REACH a turning point. I will not tell you that it will be easy, but I will tell you that it is well worth it. A decision is needed to do this that must be made over and over. It is to face your fears. After all, OCD is a fear based illness.

In the Bible Joshua and Caleb were an example of this turning point. They faced the same fear as the rest of the Israelites, but handled it differently. Let's look at it together and see what it has to do with obsessive compulsive disorder.

The Lord said to Moses, "Send some men to explore the land of Canaan, which I am giving to the Israelites. From each ancestral tribe send one of its leaders." So at the Lord's command Moses sent them out from the Desert of Paran. All of them were leaders of the Israelites. These are their names: from the tribe of Reuben, Shammua son of Zakkur; from the tribe of Simeon, Shaphat son of Hori; from the tribe of Judah, Caleb son of Jephunneh; from the tribe of Issachar, Igal son of Joseph; from the tribe of Ephraim, Hoshea son of Nun; from the tribe of Benjamin, Palti son of Raphu; from the tribe of Zebulun, Gaddiel son of Sodi; from the tribe of Manasseh (a tribe of Joseph), Gaddi son of Susi; from the tribe of Dan, Ammiel son of Gemalli; from the tribe of Asher, Sethur son of Michael; from the tribe of Naphtali, Nahbi son of Vophsi; from the tribe of Gad, Geuel son of Maki. These are the names of the men Moses sent to explore the land. (Moses gave Hoshea son of Nun the name Joshua.) When Moses sent them to explore Canaan, he said, "Go up through the Negev and on into the hill country. See what the land is like and whether the people who live there are strong or weak, few or many. What kind of land do they live in? Is it good or bad? What kind of towns do they live in? Are they unwalled or fortified? How is the soil? Is it fertile or poor? Are there trees in it or not?

Do your best to bring back some of the fruit of the land." (It was the season for the first ripe grapes. Numbers 13:1-19)

    1.   How many men did God want Moses to pick?

    2.   What was the mission of these men?

Then Caleb silenced the people before Moses and said, "We should go up and take possession of the land, for we can certainly do it." But the men who had gone up with him said, "We can't attack those people; they are stronger than we are." Numbers 13:30-31

    1.   What did Caleb and Joshua say about the land?

    2.   What did the other ten men say about the land?

The Israelites believed the report of the ten scouts instead of the report of Joshua and Caleb. This was a defining moment as God decided that generation of Israelites were not going to inherit the Promised Land except for Joshua and Caleb. The ten scouts and the Israelites were too fearful the first time around.

At this point, I need to be clear. Your promised land is overcoming obsessive compulsive disorder. The thing that will keep you from getting better or getting better quicker is fear. You will have to face your fears.

The Israelites who did not go into the Promised Land wondered in circles in the desert until they all died, and a new generation with the leadership of Joshua and Caleb inherited. I must admit here that I wondered in what I felt like was circles with OCD. It was also because I did not want to face my fears, but wanted to avoid them.

You must choose to be a Joshua or Caleb when it comes to your promised land of improvement with OCD. I like the words that God encouraged Joshua with as he was leading the new generation into the Promised Land.

Be strong and courageous, because you will lead these people to inherit the land I swore to their ancestors to give them. Joshua 1:6

Be strong and very courageous. Be careful to obey all the law my servant Moses gave you; do not turn from it to the right or to the left, that you may be successful wherever you go. Joshua 1:7

Have I not commanded you? Be strong and courageous. Do not be afraid; do not be discouraged, for the Lord your God will be with you wherever you go. Joshua 1:9

…Only be strong and courageous. Joshua 1:18

1. ***What is the one consistent statement that God made to Joshua over and over?***

2. ***What promise did God makes Joshua in Joshua 1:9?***

The same words that apply to Joshua apply to you as you make the turning point to inherit your promised land of overcoming obsessive compulsive disorder.

BE STRONG AND COURAGEOUS.

WHY?

GOD IS WITH YOU AS YOU DO IT.

I encourage you to use the following statement as you face the fears or triggers that OCD presents. I said it this way in my journey...

"I'm going into my promised land and inherit it by faith."

Write that statement out a few times below...

_____

_____

_____

Now, start using it in your battle and remember what Joshua was told by God!

CHAPTER 3

Scouting Out the Land

THE LORD TOLD Moses to send the scouts into the Promised Land to see what it was like. We are going into the territory of OCD to explore it. This exploration will help you understand it and face it as we progress. Ready to scout it out? Be a brave Joshua and Caleb. You need to know the land you are going to conquer with God's help!

Sometimes resources made to assist people with obsessive compulsive disorder are complex and do not keep the process simple enough that it can be understood. It is my goal to make this as easy as I can.

WHAT IS OBSESSIVE COMPULSIVE DISORDER?

It may feel like you are alone in dealing with it, but you are not. You are just not aware how many people around you could have it as they sometimes do not speak up about it. It is curious that in the United States alone, 1 in 40 adults have OCD and 1 in 100 children do.[1]

The disorder is made up of two components.

Obsessions are persistent unwanted thoughts that are disturbing to the one who has them and results in anxiety or fear.

Compulsions are repetitive actions or mental routines one goes through in an attempt to prevent or reduce anxiety and fear caused by the obsession.

I am now going to give some examples of obsessions and compulsions for you to think about and identify what the person is experiencing. This identification can help you in your own identification later.

Mark's Obsessive Compulsive Disorder Case

Mark was 23 years old and full of life. He had graduated from a university in Oklahoma with a business degree that landed him an executive position in a company that was a dream come true. He had a secret that he was keeping from his family, girlfriend, and co-workers. It all started one morning while he was getting ready for work and then spiraled out of control gradually. Mark wondered lots of things as he was trying to leave for his job. Did he lock the front door? Did he leave a window open? Did he leave the stove on after cooking breakfast? Was the coffee pot turned off? What about the iron that he used to press his shirt? The thoughts were so persistent about things being left on or things left open that it took great effort to get to work. Guys are known for being able to get ready fast, but it was no longer the case for Mark. The hour preparation time to get to work turned into two hours or more. Why? One hour was needed to check numerous times if things were left on or open. The thoughts of things left on or open even carried into the workplace as he often felt things were still left undone. Some days the idea of things such as the front door being open or the iron possibly burning down the house resulted in a lunch hour being spent checking it all out again just like the morning process was not enough. He hoped that it would not get worse and possibly cost him his dream job or his girlfriend. In a last ditch effort, he started even recording on his cell phone a memo all that had been locked and turned off just before he left for work. If he felt it was necessary to remove an anxiety at work about things being open or on, he would excuse himself to the bathroom and listen to the recording.

1. What were Mark's obsessions?

2. *What were Mark's compulsions?*

Macy's Obsessive Compulsive Disorder Case

She was a 32 year old stay at home mom. Her two children Ryan who was 3 and Sara who was 5 were her pride and joy. One day the thought came to mind that she and her family might get Malaria. Macy did not want anything to happen like that as her husband and kids meant more than words could express. She knew that Malaria was not something she needed to be concerned about, but the thought persisted. It motivated her to start to clean the home more than normal. She could spend hours scrubbing, mopping, and wiping daily. This surely would keep her family safe. In the beginning, the hours of daily cleaning seemed to ease her fears about Malaria, but then she felt that it was also necessary to wash her hands and shower after cleaning due to the fact she might have Malaria germs. The hand washing became something that happened throughout the day and showering went from what would be considered routine to extreme. Macy's husband could not reach her one day and thought something might be wrong. He came home at lunch and found her in the shower and the kids were playing in the bedroom beside it. She could no longer hide it from her husband as he had also noticed the electrical and water bill had been rising.

1. *What was Macy's obsession?*

2. *What were Macy's compulsions?*

Richard's Obsessive Compulsive Disorder Case

Richard was 51 years old with what would be considered a wonderful family. He worked as a bank president and was a hands on dad to his four kids Travis, Sherry, Matt, and Kevin. Two of the boys were in college and two of the kids were still at home. He was involved in their sports activities, often as their coach or assistant coach. Richard and his family were also known for vacationing due to the great value placed upon family. It was on one of these vacations that he was startled. All of them were crossing a bridge by foot and the thought entered his mind to push someone else off the bridge. This shocked him. He would never do anything like that. As time passed, other thoughts began to scare him. He would be using a knife and have the thought to stab someone with it. These thoughts disturbed him so much that he started to avoid walking to high places with others and also let others use the knives to work in the kitchen instead. Richard made sure all the knives were put up and could not be seen. Seeing one caused anxiety. His wife and kids did not understand why the dad who used to ride roller coasters now liked to sit on a bench and wait for them. Little did they know he could not bear the unwanted thoughts of pushing them or someone else off the stairs or ramps.

1. *What were Richard's obsessions?*

2. *What were Richard's compulsions?*

What are common obsessions?

- Obsessions about coming into contact with germs, cleaning agents, pesticides, or chemicals
- Obsessions about getting sick from what are considered contaminated people, places, or items
- Obsessions of harming another person by an action
- Obsessions of something bad happening to someone else if the person with OCD does not do some particular action
- Obsessions of harming oneself
- Obsession that things have to be ordered or perfect to prevent something bad from happening to others or oneself
- Obsessions about what would be considered sexually immoral
- Obsessions about hoarding objects
- Obsessions that would be considered religiously irreverent or having excessive concern for moral issues
- Obsessions that show up as questions, words, phrases, or routines
- Obsessions that certain numbers or things are lucky and other numbers or things are not

What are common compulsions?

Compulsion of washing one's hands, and sometimes people do it until they bleed or crack

Compulsion of cleaning the house in excess

Compulsion of showering in excess

Compulsion of grooming in excess

Compulsions of checking to see if things are locked or unplugged

Compulsions to see or if people or pets are alright

Compulsions of touching, tapping, rubbing, or counting in a certain way

Compulsions of mental rituals to make something feel right

Compulsion to seek reassurance

Compulsions to avoid

Compulsions to keep things (hoarding)

Compulsions to make sure things are symmetric or perfect

These lists are not exhaustive of obsessions or compulsions, but should give you an idea.

<u>Your Obsessive Compulsive Disorder Case</u>

Please take a moment to create your own case study like above. Be brave! God is with you. *Have I not commanded you? Be strong and courageous. Do not be afraid; do not be discouraged, for the Lord your God will be with you wherever you go.* Joshua 1:9 Now, pray before you do it asking for God's help. We will use it later on in the workbook. Use the space provided in this workbook, or get a piece of paper for more writing space.

Now it is time to ask some questions about your personal obsessive compulsive disorder case.

   1. *What are your obsessions?*

   2. *What are your compulsions?*

What causes Obsessive Compulsive Disorder?

What was your first vehicle? I remember my first vehicle very clearly was a 1987 Nissan Pickup. It was a burnt orange color with a black pin stripe down both sides. The thing that made it unique was the fact it was a stick shift. I had never driven a stick shift until that day I got it. As you can expect, there was a learning curve in figuring out how to drive the vehicle. The gear had 5 speeds, neutral, and reverse. I adapted pretty quickly with just a few embarrassing incidents. I know that I let off numerous times on the clutch and the gas at the wrong time and either made the truck die or squeal like I was going to do a wheelie down the street. Do not laugh; you may have done it yourself! There were also the times that I lurched forward over and over. The thing that took a little bit of time to conquer were hills. It was harder to get the clutch and gas just right. I did not want to embarrass myself and roll down a hill!

What would have happened if my gear shift would have broken in my pickup? I would have been stuck. The human brain also has a stick shift. When it is functioning properly, the ride is smooth. When the brain's stick shift gets stuck it is what we call OCD. I am getting this idea from Dr. Jeffrey Schwartz's book: <u>Brain Lock: Free Yourself from Obsessive-Compulsive Behaviour</u>.[2]

The stick shift's malfunction is related to a chemical problem in the brain. As a result the obsessions will not go away and they come like a frontal assault in a war zone. One of the main processing signal parts of the brain is made up to two structures that we will refer to as the **Caudate Nucleus** and the **Putamen**. They are your brain's stick shift!

The Caudate Nucleus coordinates with the part of the brain that helps with thinking and the Putamen coordinates with the part of the brain that helps with body movements. When the Caudate Nucleus does its job, the brain shifts gears easily to other thoughts. When the shifter gets stuck, the thoughts get stuck in the front part of the brain.

The result of all this are false messages that come as obsessions and compulsions. Compulsions come to relieve the anxiety since we are dealing with the Putamen that helps control body motions.

CHARLES THOMPSON

It also appears that there is an imbalance of neurotransmitters that are known as Serotonin and Glutamine. This is why people say that OCD is a chemical imbalance. Medication is often prescribed to try to create the best possible balance in these transmitters, often showing positive results.

Even with all of the advance scientific research available as of this writing, there are still unknown things about obsessive compulsive disorder. The disorder could be triggered by a combination of genetic, behavioral, cognitive, neurological, and environmental factors. There have been cases where it's possible that OCD could be associated with a Streptococcal infections, as it results in dysfunction and inflammation in the Basil Ganglia containing the Caudate Nucleus and Putamen.

Studies have also shown that OCD tends to run in families. It can start at any age, but does have some averages. The averages are ages 10 to 12 and 18 to 25.

I went into all the detail above to let you know that it is not as easy to deal with OCD as being told to, "Stop thinking about it!" The brain is malfunctioning just as any other part of the human body can malfunction. It is not your fault and it is not a shameful thing.

Those with obsessive compulsive disorder do not agree with or want the obsessions they are having. They are appalled by them.

1. *What did you learn about obsessive compulsive disorder that surprised you?*

2. *What did you learn about obsessive compulsive disorder that could be helpful to you now?*

CHAPTER 4

Forgiveness

ONE OF THE things that I remember about growing up in East Texas is the clay. The rain would come and usually mud formed. Clay is a little different when it is wet. As you walk around, it collects on the bottom of your feet and sticks. As you collect more, you get taller! The East Texas way of removing the clay is to use a stick and scrape it off.

I have also found that in walking through life there is something else that can collect on your feet. What is it? It is anger and bitterness that builds when not choosing to forgive others who have hurt you in the past. These emotional scars fester and can make having OCD worse.

I did not have the easiest childhood and did not handle it in the best way. I can tell you from personal experience that the bitterness made my violent, religious, or contamination obsessions worse than they should have been.

We must take the stick of the Word of God and obey to scrape it off. Bitterness effects the emotions and obsessive compulsive disorder toys with them as well.

1. *Do you think in your personal experience that unforgiveness, bitterness, and anger have made obsessive compulsive disorder harder for you?*

   YES   NO

Let's take a moment to examine forgiving others.

Jesus served as our example of forgiving others as He hung upon the cross.

Jesus said, "Father, forgive them, for they do not know what they are doing." And they divided up his clothes by casting lots. Luke 23:34

From my human logic, I would think that the men nailing Him on the cross knew exactly what they were doing with every whip, blow, and pound. Jesus said that if they really knew what they were doing, they would not have done it. The same applies to those who hurt us, if they really knew what they were doing to us, they would not do it. The Lord forgave upon the cross and He compels us to do the same.

Get rid of all bitterness, rage and anger, brawling and slander, along with every form of malice. Be kind and compassionate to one another, forgiving each other, just as in Christ God forgave you. Ephesians 4:31-32

1. *What does this passage say to get rid of?*

2. *What does this passage say about forgiving others?*

Bear with each other and forgive one another if any of you has a grievance against someone. Forgive as the Lord forgave you. Colossians 3:13

1. *Why does bearing with one another help prevent any bitterness from setting in?*

2. What does this passage say about forgiving others?

The forgiveness we have as believers came through love and grace. He loved us first by being willing to die for us and offer us salvation. He offered us salvation, a free gift to accept, that we could never earn. The moment of our salvation, God forgave us of our past, present, and future sins.

With all of this in mind, we should use it to frame how to forgive others.

We need to take the initiative by loving first to forgive others. We cannot wait until they ask for forgiveness or clean up their act.

We need to show them grace by showing them forgiveness as a free gift. They do not have to earn it.

Forgiving others is a choice. It is to agree with God and do it no matter how we feel. It is to appreciate the unconditional love and forgiveness we have in Christ Jesus and to extend it to others as His example.

It does not mean that you have to let them hurt you again, but it does mean to forgive in obedience, because if you do not, they are still hurting you anyway, as you are full of anger and bitterness.

How many times do you forgive someone? A discussion between Jesus and the Apostle Peter is revealing about this.

Then Peter came to Jesus and asked, "Lord, how many times shall I forgive my brother or sister who sins against me? Up to seven times?" Jesus answered, "I tell you, not seven times, but seventy-seven times." Matthew 18:21-22

Peter thought he was doing very well if someone did something to him seven times one day and forgave them. Jesus had a higher standard, if a person does the same thing to you 490 times in one day, you forgive them every time. There is no way that a person can do the same thing to you that many times in one day. The essence of the illustration is that we are to forgive unlimited.

It may be necessary to remove yourself from the situation or take a time out if a person does it over and over.

1. *What experiences have you been through that could have caused you to pick up some bitterness and the need to forgive other people?*

Please ask God to reveal to you if there is any situation that fits this and write it in the space provided until you know it is complete above.

2. *What people do you need to forgive?*

Please ask God to reveal them to you and write their names above in the space provided.

Now that you have done the faithful work of examining your life, let's put it into practice.

For every person you need to forgive, plug in their name and pray the following prayer. Also include what they did to you in order to release the burden you have been carrying.

Jesus, I follow your example and choose to forgive _____ for _____. Heal my emotional scars and any damage that was done as I release the individual to You.

There is one last thing to address with forgiveness. Just as clay collects on the bottom of shoes, forgiving is an ongoing process. You should forgive others every day to clean up and also the same person every time they hurt you if needed.

CHAPTER 5

This Means War

S PIRITUAL BATTLES TAKE place behind the scene where the human eye does not see. I also believe and know firsthand that spiritual battles take place with obsessive compulsive disorder. The enemy of our soul tries to take advantage of the disorder and succeeds only if we let him do so. It is a point of weakness and it only makes sense he would attack a point of weakness.

1. *How do you think that the enemy tries to take advantage of a person who has OCD?*

2. *How do you think the enemy has attacked you using your OCD as a point of weakness?*

Every believer has been equipped with the armor of God to be able to stand his or her ground in a spiritual battle. Each of the unique pieces has a part to play in winning the spiritual battle that can happen with OCD.

It is now time to discuss how to fight in a spiritual battle involving obsessive compulsive disorder. It is time for you to fight back with God's help and win!

10 Finally, be strong in the Lord and in his mighty power. 11 Put on the full armor of God, so that you can take your stand against the devil's schemes. 12 For our struggle is not against flesh and blood, but against the rulers, against the authorities, against the powers of this dark world and against the spiritual forces of evil in the heavenly realms. 13 Therefore put on the full armor of God, so that when the day of evil comes, you may be able to stand your ground, and after you have done everything, to stand. 14 Stand firm then, with the belt of truth buckled around your waist, with the breastplate of righteousness in place, 15 and with your feet fitted with the readiness that comes from the gospel of peace. 16 In addition to all this, take up the shield of faith, with which you can extinguish all the flaming arrows of the evil one. 17 Take the helmet of salvation and the sword of the Spirit, which is the word of God.18 And pray in the Spirit on all occasions with all kinds of prayers and requests. With this in mind, be alert and always keep on praying for all the Lord's people. Ephesians 6:10-18

The Apostle Paul makes it very clear that it is not our personal strength that will win a spiritual battle, but the Lord's mighty power (v10). This is something you have to grasp with spiritual battles involving OCD. You do not have what it takes to defeat the enemy when he attacks your point of weakness. The wonderful news is that the Lord is up to the battle! He will vanquish the enemy.

1. *How much of the armor of God are we supposed to put on during a spiritual battle (v11)?*

2. *What will you be able to do when you put on the full armor of God in a spiritual battle (v13)?*

We will examine each part of the armor now.

Obsessive Compulsive Disorder and the Belt of Truth (v14)

There are lots of lies involved in the process of spiritual battles with OCD.

The first lie comes from OCD itself.

The story is told of Howard Hughes not being able to eat off of the same plate after using it once as it was viewed as contaminated. The plate was destroyed.

   1.   *What was the lie of obsessive compulsive disorder?*

   2.   *What was the truth about the plates he ate off of?*

The second set of lies come from the enemy. He is called the accuser of believers in Revelation 12:10.

The enemy will tell you that you are worthless, you should take your life, you are hopeless, you cannot get better, you did this to yourself, and many more possible things.

   1.   *What are some of the lies the enemy tells you that are related to your OCD?*

2. *What are the truths that you need to use to discard the lies you have been told?*

Then you will know the truth, and the truth will set you free. John 8:32

<u>Obsessive Compulsive Disorder and the Breastplate of Righteousness (v14)</u>

1. *How righteous are you?*

Righteousness and holiness are not to be confused with each other. Righteousness is who you are and holiness is what you do.

When you were an unbeliever, the Bible describes your righteousness in the following terms.

All of us have become like one who is unclean, and all our righteous acts are like filthy rags; we all shrivel up like a leaf, and like the wind our sins sweep us away. Isaiah 64:6

Filthy rag…got it? There was no way that you could earn heaven or be good enough to get in.

Jesus changed all this in what He did at the cross and what He gave you when you became a Christian.

For if, by the trespass of the one man, death reigned through that one man, how much more will those who receive God's abundant provision of grace and of the gift of righteousness reign in life through the one man, Jesus Christ. Romans 5:17

The righteousness of Christ has been given to you as a free gift.

Let us get real for a moment. OCD can sometimes make people feel worthless. The thoughts can be so offensive it is hard not to take it personally. God knows that you do not want those thoughts and is also able to separate you from them. He knows the real you. You cannot be held accountable for thoughts that are not you and do not want to begin with. He sees your heart after Him. You need to be able to say, "It's OCD", because God clearly knows it is.

You are not your obsessions. It is His grace that saved you and it is His grace that will keep you. You could not save yourself and cannot keep yourself saved. You can relax in His grace. He is your righteousness. You were never righteous enough in your own self effort to get into heaven and never will be. It is a gift.

1. *How does it make you feel to know that God is able to see you separate from obsessive compulsive disorder?*

2. *How does it make you feel to know you are permanently covered in Christ's righteousness as a gift?*

Obsessive Compulsive Disorder and the Gospel of Peace(v15)

Jesus made a profound statement…

Peace I leave with you; my peace I give you. I do not give to you as the world gives. Do not let your hearts be troubled and do not be afraid. John 14:27

He does not want our hearts troubled or afraid. He offers a peace that the world does not offer, if we find ourselves lacking. This is beautiful news for someone who struggles with anxiety.

The believer has access to a peace that the unbeliever does not. We are invited to approach Him and take hold of what He offers.

It all starts with a choice.

Do not be anxious about anything, but in every situation, by prayer and petition, with thanksgiving, present your requests to God. And the peace of God, which transcends all understanding, will guard your hearts and your minds in Christ Jesus. Philippians 4:6-7

1. *What does God want us to do when we find ourselves anxious?*

2. *What is the result of doing this?*

This will be discussed further in the section on prayer and obsessive compulsive disorder.

Obsessive Compulsive Disorder and the Shield of Faith (v16)

The shield described in this passage is one that could cover the whole body of a soldier. What activates this shield? Faith. It is faith in God.

In the midst of a spiritual battle with obsessive compulsive disorder, it is easy to take hold of fear and run with it. This is when you have to choose to believe that God will fulfill the promises and plan He has for you.

I am convinced and confident of this very thing, that He who has begun a good work in you will [continue to] perfect and complete it until the day of Christ Jesus [the time of His return]. Philippians 1:6, Amplified Bible

1. **What promise has God made to you in this passage?**

2. **What can you believe when it comes to life and OCD from reading this passage?**

And we know that in all things God works for the good of those who love him, who have been called according to his purpose. Romans 8:28

1. **What promise has God made you in this verse in regards to having OCD?**

2. **How does this make you feel?**

…For He has said, "I will never [under any circumstances] desert you [nor give you up nor leave you without support, nor will I in any degree leave you helpless], nor will I forsake or let you down or relax My hold on you [assuredly not]!" 6 So we take comfort and are encouraged and confidently say, "The Lord is my Helper [in time of need], I will not be afraid. What will man do to me. Hebrews 13:5b-6, Amplified Bible

1. ***What promise does God make to you in this passage?***

2. ***What faith can you have because of this promise when struggling with obsessive compulsive disorder?***

Fear will say, "It is over." Faith will say, "God will complete what He started in me." Fear will say, "It is hopeless." Faith will say, "God will work this out to my good!" Fear will say, "You are all alone!" Faith will say, "God is with me forever and will help me."

Trust in the Lord with all your heart and lean not on your own understanding; in all your ways submit to him, and he will make your paths straight. Proverbs 3:5-6

There will be times I personally say to God, "I give you the responsibility for obsessive compulsive disorder." It involves admitting I cannot control OCD and entrust it to Him.

Obsessive Compulsive Disorder and the Helmet of Salvation (v17)

OCD has been compared to a gear shift that gets stuck in the brain as the thought will not go away and it must be manually shifted as a result.[3]

The helmet protected the head of the solider and it is meant to protect your head as well when it comes to obsessive compulsive disorder.

The obsession or compulsion must be captured.

For though we live in the world, we do not wage war as the world does. The weapons we fight with are not the weapons of the world. On the contrary, they have divine power to demolish strongholds. We demolish arguments and every pretension that sets itself up against the knowledge of God, and we TAKE CAPTIVE every thought to make it obedient to Christ. And we will be ready to punish every act of disobedience, once your obedience is complete. 2 Corinthians 10:3-6

> 1. *How can you take an obsessive thought captive?*

> 2. *How can you take a compulsion captive?*

The obsession or compulsion you have is not inevitable as you have an escape route.

No temptation has overtaken you except what is common to mankind. And God is faithful; he will not let you be tempted beyond what you can bear. But when you are tempted, he will also provide a way out so that you can endure it. 1 Corinthians 10:13

This passage can apply to those of us who have OCD.

Temptation is common to mankind and so is obsessive compulsive disorder, as we have discussed before. You are not the only one who has it.

1. *How does this encourage you?*

God is faithful to us in tempting times and He will also be faithful to us when we are facing obsessions or compulsions. He will not say tough, handle it yourself.

1. *How does this encourage you?*

He always leaves us a way out to avoid sinning, and that applies to OCD as well. He will leave us a way out; for we do not have to act on obsessions and compulsions.

1. *What are the ways out from an obsession?*

2. *What are the ways out from a compulsion?*

We must learn to depend upon God and take these ways out or the vicious cycle of obsessions and compulsions will have us going in circles or immobilize us at times.

Obsessive Compulsive Disorder and the Sword of the Holy Spirit (v17)

This is a reference to the Bible. It is full of wonderful passages that can build us up when it comes to dealing with obsessive compulsive disorder.

It is helpful to write a passage down or memorize it to use in a time of need when dealing with obsessions, compulsions, or anxiety. The Word of God can help shift the gear of what is stuck in our brain.

Some of the passages that you could look at are Psalm 23 and Psalm 91. You can take a part of it or use the whole.

The Bible can benefit us as it is living and active.

For the word of God is living and active and full of power [making it operative, energizing, and effective]. It is sharper than any two-edged sword, penetrating as far as the division of the soul and spirit [the completeness of a person], and of both joints and marrow [the deepest parts of our nature], exposing and judging the very thoughts and intentions of the heart. Hebrews 4:12, Amplified Bible

1. *Can you think of a verse or passage that can help you?*

Write it on a note card to carry in your pocket or memorize it.

Obsessive Compulsive Disorder and Prayer (v18)

Prayer is mere communication with God. He not only listens to us, but is also willing to speak back.

1. *What is your prayer life like?*

2. *What can you do to use it to overcome OCD?*

I am going to save this exciting part of the armor of God for the next chapter and devote a whole section alone. I think you are ready for war with God's help to take on OCD and the enemy too!

CHAPTER 6

The Power of Prayer

I WANT YOU TO know that this is one of the areas that has helped me the most with obsessive compulsive disorder and rendered an untold amount of benefits. It excites me to share it with you.

If any of you lacks wisdom, you should ask God, who gives generously to all without finding fault, and it will be given to you. James 1:5

1. Who does this verse say that we can ask for?

2. How willing does the verse say He is to give us wisdom?

If there was any time that you needed wisdom, it would be while personally dealing with obsessions or compulsions. God sees obsessions and compulsions differently than we see them.

God eagerly wants to be a part of dealing with OCD and you are able to hear Him in the middle of it. He can help you break the cycle of an obsession or a compulsion. Prayer can help with triggers that come too.

When do you do it?

Do not let your hearts be troubled.... John 14:1a

You need to talk to God anytime you experience the trouble of obsessions, compulsions, fear, or anxiety.

What do you say?

Here is a list of ideal things you can ask God in the middle of dealing with obsessions or compulsions.

Father, what is this really about?

Jesus, what are you teaching me?

God, how do you want me to respond to this?

Father, what do you want to tell me?

What does my heart need to hear from you right now?

After doing this, wait until you hear from Him. He will most likely speak to you internally. You may need to ask again if you are not calm enough at the beginning or were distracted.

What do you do now?

Once you have heard from God, then there are several more steps to take.

1. Humbly take any action that He desires for you to take.

2. Renounce any lie that you have believed.

3. Repent of any sin that He may desire for you to address to further the breakthrough.

4. Ask Him to speak to you a truth you need to hear.

5. Rejoice in Him about all that you have received.

Please allow me a moment to put this into practice for you. My OCD is triggered sometimes while reading.

I notice immediately that it is OCD. Why? Anxiety.

I stop and ask God what this is about? I listen.

Most of the time I am made aware of some untrue obsession I have.

I repent for coming into agreement with it and renounce it.

I ask God what truth I need to know. I listen.

It usually is the opposite of the lie and brings freedom.

Now, I thank Him for helping me.

This is a process that is going to become very important to overcoming OCD. You need to memorize or write down these steps and start using them. You will learn to hear God clearer and clearer while praying this way. You will also start to have a smile across your face more often.

CHAPTER 7

Medication and Counseling

T HE CHRISTIAN LIFE needs balance. The reality is that you have obsessive compulsive disorder and you need help. You must now get over the: **I have it under control and the I do not need anyone else**.

OCD is an illness. You are not going crazy and it is highly treatable. There is no shame in opening up about what you are going through.

I think one of the first places you need to open up is with God. We have been discussing this along the way. He loves you.

In the Old Testament He healed people and He also did in the New Testament. As a matter of fact, Hebrews 13:8 says, *Jesus Christ is the same yesterday and today and forever.*

In the Old Testament, Isaiah declared, *But He was wounded for our transgressions, He was crushed for our wickedness [our sin, our injustice, our wrongdoing]; The punishment [required] for our well-being fell on Him, And by His stripes (wounds) we are healed.* Isaiah 53:5, Amplified Bible

This passage foretold that Jesus would die for our sins in order to bring forgiveness and the stripes to be laid across His back would bring physical healing.

He himself bore our sins in his body on the cross, so that we might die to sins and live for righteousness; by his wounds you have been healed. 1 Peter 2:24

The Apostle Peter confirmed that those words are something Jesus did and still does today. With all that said, I point you to Jesus.

I have asked Him to heal my body and I encourage you to do the same. Leave the results to Him and just love Him. I have resolved to serve Him with all my heart healed or not healed.

Do you have any close and personal Christian friends? I would encourage you to ask them to pray for you in regards to healing. *And these signs will accompany those who believe: In my name they will…place their hands on sick people, and they will get well.* Mark 16:17a, 18b These are the type of people you can open up to and ask them as many times as you want to believe for healing, while laying hands on you in prayer. You should also take into mind obeying James 5:14-15a, *Is anyone among you sick? Let them call the elders of the church to pray over them and anoint them with oil in the name of the Lord. And the prayer offered in faith will make the sick person well.*

I said all those things to let you know that I do believe in miracles. I also believe in doctors and medicine too.

God is the One who gave the doctors and the creators of medications the ability to do what they do. Did you know that God used someone to write the Bible who was a doctor?

Luke, the beloved physician… Colossians 4:14a

He was used to write the book of Luke and the book of Acts.

God uses people to help people. In the parable of the good Samaritan, he tended to the wounds of the one who had been robbed.

Doctors and medication can tend to our needs.

There are four types of people you can see who are professionals when it comes to OCD.

Psychiatrist - A physician who practices the science of diagnosing and treating mental disorders. He or she may write prescriptions too.[4]

Psychologist – A specialist who understands the mind, mental states, and processes.[5]

Therapist – A person trained in the use of psychological methods for helping patients overcome psychological problems.[6]

Counselor – A person who gives instructions, advice, or opinions to help another person.[7]

I personally have seen all of the above, and they have been beneficial to me. They have understanding that I do not have and are familiar with things I am not.

For lack of guidance a nation falls, but victory is won through many advisers. Proverbs 11:14

There could be some victory God brings through using professionals in your life.

1. *What do you think about seeking professional help?*

I would make God part of this process of choosing help. I would also recommend trying to find Christian professionals if you can, but if not, secular ones can provide success too. It is nice to see a Christian professional as they share your faith. Of all the professionals available, the one most important to have as a believer, is the counselor. You want to get Biblical direction, instead of worldly, that could be misleading.

I have also been on medication since I was young for obsessive compulsive disorder. I have truly been able to tell the difference with it. The following is a list from WebMd of common medications for the disorder.

Lexapro
Zoloft
Celexa
Prozac
Citalopram
Paxil CR
Paxil
Sertraline
Risperdal
Fluoxetine
Paroxetine
Risperidone
Escitalopram oxalate
Pexeva
Clomipramine
Anafranil
Fluvoxamine
Sarafem
Risperdal M-TAB
Paroxetine mesylate[8]

How does medication work? The medications used to treat OCD are usually antidepressants and they specifically work with a chemical in the brain called serotonin. The goal is to balance the serotonin and thus improve the symptoms of obsessions and compulsions. These drugs are also called selective serotonin reuptake inhibitors or SSRI's. Your physician may prescribe these or may add some additional drugs not present in this list. These drugs may be for a period of time or they may be for a lifetime. Unless God tells me otherwise, I am on medication for a lifetime.

In short, this action helps with obsessions, compulsions, and anxiety. Medication is no cure at this point, but it can be beneficial. Often, it takes about three months to know if a medication is going to work and if it is the right one for you. It may take some adjustments of doses or even a different medication to get it right. There is also a possibility that one may not agree with you, and you will need another one that has no side effects.

The medication that I take is Luvox. It is available in a generic form and so are many of the other medications to cut down cost. There are also drug discount cards available for free on the internet that can cut the cost of medication.

CHAPTER 8

Identity Theft

THE UNITED STATES Bureau of Justice defines identity theft in three distinct ways.[9] First, it is the unauthorized use or attempted use of an existing account. Next, it is the unauthorized use or attempted use of personal information to open a new account. Lastly, it is the misuse of personal information for a fraudulent purpose. The latest report of identity theft was done in 2014 and says that 17.6 million United States residents were the victims that year.

I have been the victim of identity theft before on numerous times by someone using my bank debit card unauthorized. Have you? It made me mad. I have also been the victim of a different type of identity theft. Obsessive compulsive disorder has tried numerous times to take my identity. It makes me feel like I AM OCD.

It sounds like this if I was to put it into words….

I am a failure as a husband due to OCD.

I am a failure as a dad due to OCD.

I am a failure as a minister due to OCD.

I am a failure as a Christian because of OCD.

Those are all examples of OCD trying to hijack my identity.

1. **Take a moment to write down the various ways obsessive compulsive disorder tries to hi-jack your identity below.**

You will feel defeated if you let OCD take over your identity. I have one word for what OCD says to me in trying to hack, "Lies". It is all lies!

I am not obsessive compulsive disorder. It does not define me. It is not my identity.

I am Charles Thompson.

You are _____ (write your first and last name), and not obsessive compulsive disorder.

Say the above sentence out loud!

So God created mankind in his own image, in the image of God he created them; male and female he created them. Genesis 1:27

1. *Whose image are you made in according to this verse?*

2. *How does that give you great value?*

Your identity comes from your Creator. It does not come from anything you do or do not do. It is not your job, failures, successes, problems, or illnesses. As long as you let those things define you, there will be a rough roller coaster ride of long emotional ups and downs.

Just in case you do not believe me about OCD not being your identity, let's look at other illnesses.

I am heart disease. People with heart diseases do not call themselves that.

I am diabetes. People with diabetes do not walk around and say, "My name is diabetes, what is your name sir?"

An illness is just a mere tiny part of you.

We are of great value because God made us, and we have unique personalities, strengths, talents, and much more! You have a disorder, you are not a disorder.

God also has a plan for our life.

13 For you created my inmost being; you knit me together in my mother's womb. 14 I praise you because I am fearfully and wonderfully made; your works are wonderful, I know that full well.15 My frame was not hidden from you when I was made in the secret place, when I was woven together in the depths of the earth.16 Your eyes saw my unformed body; all the days ordained for me were written in your book before one of them came to be.17 How precious to me are your thoughts, God! How vast is the sum of them!18 Were I to count them, they would outnumber the grains of sand—when I awake, I am still with you. Psalms 139:13-18

1. Who put you together according to Psalms 139:13?

2. How are you made according to Psalms 139:14?

3. How much ahead of time did God have a plan for you according to Psalms 139:16?

4. How many good thoughts does God have about you according to Psalms 139:17–18?

For I know the plans I have for you," declares the Lord, "plans to prosper you and not to harm you, plans to give you hope and a future. Jeremiah 29:11

1. What type of plan does God have for your life?

2. How can this encourage you?

And we know that in all things God works for the good of those who love him, who have been called according to his purpose. Romans 8:28

1. *What does God promise to do with this thing called OCD?*

Now, let's get back to your identity. Who are you as a Christian? What does God say? That is all that matters.

Who I Am In Christ[10]

I AM NOT obsessive compulsive disorder, I AM ACCEPTED...
I am God's child (John 1:12)
I am a friend of Christ (John 15:15)
I am justified and declared righteous (Romans 5:1)
I am united with the Lord (1 Corinthians 6:17)
I am bought with a price and belong to God (1 Corinthians 6:19-20)
I am chosen by God and adopted as His child (Ephesians 1:3-8)
I am redeemed and forgiven of all my sins (Colossians 1:13-14)
I am complete in Christ (Colossians 2:9-10)
I am able to come directly to the throne of grace through Christ (Hebrews 4:14-16)

I AM NOT obsessive compulsive disorder, I AM SECURE...
I am free from condemnation (Romans 8:1-2)
I am assured that God works all circumstances to my good (Romans 8:28)
I am not able to be separated from the love of God (Romans 8:31-39)
I am established, anointed, and sealed by God (2 Corinthians 1:21-22)
I am hidden with Christ in God (Colossians 3:1-4)
I am confident Christ will finish the good work He started in me (Philippians 1:6)
I am a citizen of heaven (Philippians 3:20)
I am able to be courageous instead of fearful (2 Timothy 1:7)
I am born of God and the evil one cannot touch me (1 John 5:18)

I AM NOT obsessive compulsive disorder, I AM SIGNIFICANT...
I am a branch of Christ who is the vine (John 15:5)
I am chosen and appointed to bear fruit (John 15:16)
I am God's temple (1 Corinthians 3:16)
I am a minister of reconciliation for God (2 Corinthians 5:17-21)
I am seated with Christ in the heavenly realm (Ephesians 2:6)
I am God's workmanship (Ephesians 2:10)

I am able to approach God with freedom and confidence (Ephesians 3:12)

I am able to do all things through Christ who strengthens me (Philippians 4:13)

1. *Which one of the "you are accepted" statements stands out to you in comparison to how obsessive compulsive disorder makes you feel unacceptable?*

2. *Which one of the "you are secure" statements stands out to you in comparison to how obsessive compulsive disorder makes you feel insecure?*

3. *Which one of the "you are significant" statements stands out to you in comparison to how obsessive compulsive disorder makes you feel insignificant?*

The above statements about who you are in Christ state your identity instead of the hacking that OCD attempts. They say that a habit can take at least two weeks to develop. It might be helpful to read these out loud either before you start your day, during, or as you are going to bed for two weeks to start to replace obsessive compulsive disorders' false identity.

CHAPTER 9

Taking Thoughts Captive

H OMES HAVE A wonderful thing called air-conditioning. It is very helpful in the East Texas summers that come and go. The air-conditioner does require some maintenance to function properly. The air filters have to be checked to see if they are clean or not. The air-conditioner does not work as good when the filters are dirty and also may experience some type of breakdown eventually.

OCD is a little similar to air-conditioning. The mind is a wonderful thing that you and I have been given. It requires some maintenance to function properly. A filter is needed for someone who has OCD.

The filter works by us starting to recognize obsessive compulsive disorder's thought patterns and also taking them captive. The more we filter, the more easily our mind will work. We want to be able to say, "That is an obsessive thought!" We want to be able to identify, "That is a compulsion!"

What stuff does our mental filter need to capture?

For though we live in the world, we do not wage war as the world does. The weapons we fight with are not the weapons of the world. On the contrary, they have divine power to demolish strongholds. We demolish arguments and every pretension that sets itself up against the knowledge of God, and we TAKE CAPTIVE every thought to make it obedient to Christ. And we will be ready to punish every act of disobedience, once your obedience is complete. (2 Corinthians 10:3-6).

The following are fourteen different thinking errors common with obsessive compulsive disorder as presented by PHD John Arden and PSY Daniel Dal Corso.[11] I am thankful for Dr. John Arden giving permission to use his work in my workbook. Please be thinking about your personal OCD as your read through them and see which thinking errors you have.

1. **"Either or" Thinking** – You think things are right or wrong, clean or contaminated, safe or dangerous, black or white. This type of thinking error does not leave room for gray. Because things are not always completely right, clean, or safe. This type of thinking leads to feeling anxious. It will also lead to the desire to ritualize in order to reduce tension. The following would be examples of either or thinking. "If the mirror hangs perfectly straight, I will feel good. If it is crooked, I will feel bad until I fix it." "If I do not put my clothes on in the right sequence, I cannot leave the house."

2. **Overestimating the Probability of Risk** – This is when someone imagines that if something will go wrong, it will go wrong. Low-probability events are interpreted as high-probability events incorrectly. The following are examples of overestimating thinking. "I forgot to lock the second story windows, a thief will get in." "I need to check my son's food extra carefully to make sure no broken glass got in it." "My boss wanted to see me, so I must be facing termination."

3. **Catastrophizing or Overestimating the Severity of Risk** – This involves turning situations or circumstances into worst case scenarios. Here are some examples for you take into mind of this error thinking. "The man in the elevator coughed, so he probably has tuberculosis and I have it now." "I used a public restroom. Someone with HIV sat on it and I need to be tested now." "I think I left the toaster plugged in. My family is in danger unless I go home and unplug it!" This thinking error and the overestimating the probability of risk often work hand in hand.

4. **Emotional Reasoning** – This is when emotion is believed to be evidence of the truth, instead of checking into the facts. How you feel internally gets mistaken for external reality. The problem is these gut feelings are usually false alarms from OCD that are occurring for no particular reason. The following are some examples to consider for emotional reasoning thinking. "I have a headache. I must get to my wife's work as she must be in terrible danger." "I feel scared all of a sudden, my best friend must have been in an accident on vacation."

5. **Overgeneralizing** – Words that serve as evidence of this type of error thinking are always, never, forever, all, none, totally, none, and everyone. Some examples of this type of error are as follows. "You always do that." "I'll never get OCD under control." "I have to throw away this manual as one section triggers OCD." "I am a total failure."

6. **Superstitious Thinking** – You make connections between things and events when there is no logical reason to do it. It might be made up of implausible what if statements. This thinking increases anxiety by making causes intangible and not based on reality. Superstitious thinking is often connected to obsessions about contamination. The following are examples of superstitious thinking errors. "If I tap five times, my kid will be protected while at school." "If I hug my nephew after touching the gas pump, the germs will get on him and he will get sick." "What if the clothes I bought at the mall are contaminated because someone coughed in the bathroom and it spread into the store. I could catch a cold now."

7. **Need for Certainty or Persistent Doubting** – This error thinking is wrapped up in a lack of tolerance for uncertainty. All of us want more certainty in our lives, but people dealing with this thought distortion become anxious when there is no way to know something for sure. The need to ask questions of oneself or others to try to obtain reassurance happens. The deal

is that no matter how much is given, the doubt continues. Some examples of persistent doubting are as follows. "The doctor said my liver is fine, but I think he is wrong. I need to get a fifth opinion." "I think I locked the front door, but I am not sure. I will go back and check it." "Are you sure we did not hit a person back there? I heard a bumping noise while I was driving. I did not see anyone, should we go back?"

8. **Excessive Responsibility** – This is the thought pattern that you are responsible for everyone's safety and welfare. It includes the notion that it is possible to control the consequence of your actions. You are not in complete control of the events of your life, never have been, and will never be. You only have a certain amount of control over events. This thinking error can be represented by the following examples. "I allowed the kids to play ball outside and my nephew cut his knee. My brother will never trust me again to watch him. If the cut gets infected, it is all my fault." "My son got into trouble at school this week. I am a disaster of a parent."

9. **Overvalued Thoughts** – Thinking in this manner is the belief that if you think something, it must be true and, must mean something about you personally since you had the thought. An example this would be thinking you are a psycho because you had a thought about stabbing someone. The interpretation would be completely wrong. Value should not be assigned to such an unwanted thought caused by OCD. People with OCD believe that having unwanted violent or sexual thought makes them a bad person. Just like normal people who do not have obsessive compulsive disorder would dismiss a thought like that, we need to do so too. They dismiss and go about their day, we should too. Obsessions likewise should not be taken personally.

10. **Thought-Action Fusion** – This is the belief that thinking about something means that it happened or will cause it to happen. This line of thought puts thinking the same as doing.

The following would be examples of such thinking. "I think I pushed a man in front of that car and it hit him. I called the police and reported myself." "In a moment of anger, I wished a relative was dead. I have been praying and praying it would not happen."

11. **Perfectionism** – This error leads one to believe that everything in our control must be perfect or just so. Some people are worried that they will get into trouble for making a mistake; some cannot tolerate discomfort of things not meeting their superior standards. Examples of perfectionism would be as follows. "I have to make my bed as soon as I get up. The bedspread must hang down to the floor and have absolutely no wrinkles. If someone messes it up after I do it, I go into a panic." "I cannot send any email unless I am absolutely certain there are no typos." "I have to park perfectly in the parking space and have the bumper just over the curb." "People who have wrinkled bedspreads, sent emails with errors, and park however will have something bad happen to them."

12. **Inability to Tolerate Anxiety or Discomfort** – A person with this type of thinking believes it is never acceptable to feel uncomfortable and avoids it to prevent the feeling. Having anxiety is to be terminated instead of tolerated. In an extreme form, a person may feel they will go crazy or lose control if the anxiety continues. Examples of this error are as follows. "I have to wash my hands right now or I will go crazy." We have to go home. I cannot enjoy the show as you know how nervous I get in crowded rooms."

13. **Focusing on the Negative** – This is the belief that no matter how many things went right, the only things worth paying attention to are the ones that went wrong. When we think repeatedly about negative events and situations, our prevailing emotions are very negative. Examples of this type of error thinking are as follows. "My job evaluation was good except

one thing. I cannot stop thinking about that one thing and what a failure I am." "Everything was great until it started raining; now the day is ruined."

14. **Predicting the Future** – This is the error of thinking you know what will happen. People like this predict negative outcomes that interfere with life, making changes, and learning new things. An example of this type of thinking would be, "There is no use in trying, I will never be able to do it." It may sound like the following too, "Even though I am healthy, I know I am going to die of cancer." "There is no way that my OCD will get better."

The Bible encourages us to take control of our thoughts instead of letting them have a free for all. This would also include obsessions and compulsions.

Finally, brothers and sisters, whatever is true, whatever is noble, whatever is right, whatever is pure, whatever is lovely, whatever is admirable—if anything is excellent or praiseworthy—think about such things. Whatever you have learned or received or heard from me, or seen in me—put it into practice. And the God of peace will be with you. Philippians 4:8-9

1. *What are the things that we should direct our thoughts to according to this passage of Scripture?*

2. *How are these thoughts the opposite of obsessions and compulsions?*

The thoughts that must be captured are the ones that are the opposite of what the Apostle Paul explained. Understanding and applying the fourteen thinking errors we covered can help us identify the thoughts and make changes. Let's now look specifically at your obsessions and compulsions.

As one who has OCD, I know it can be stressful to think or write about them. You must know this is part of your recovery in being able to write about them. Face it! Do not avoid it!

Let's ask God to help us as we go forward.

"Father, I am going to face my obsessions and compulsions. I know that I am not doing this alone. You are with me. I believe that since you are with me, I can do all things through Christ who strengthens me and that includes getting better with OCD. Let my faith increase and my fear decrease as You are bigger than any fear I may face."

   1.   *What is one of your obsessive thoughts?*

   2.   *What one or two thinking errors are involved in it?*

   3.   *What is one of your compulsions?*

4. What one or two thinking errors are involved in it?

5. What do you think are your top three thinking errors out of the list of fourteen?

We now need to get a little more detailed. The whole next four pages will give the opportunity to address all your obsessions and compulsions and discover what error thinking is involved. You do not have to fill up all the charts, it is given to make sure you have enough space.

Obsessive Thoughts to Capture

My obsessive thought is…	My thinking error or errors are…
My obsessive thought is…	My thinking error or errors are…
My obsessive thought is…	My thinking error or errors are…
My obsessive thought is…	My thinking error or errors are…
My obsessive thought is…	My thinking error or errors are…
My obsessive thought is…	My thinking error or errors are…
My obsessive thought is…	My thinking error or errors are…
My obsessive thought is…	My thinking error or errors are…

CHARLES THOMPSON

Obsessive Thoughts to Capture

My obsessive thought is…	My thinking error or errors are…
My obsessive thought is…	My thinking error or errors are…
My obsessive thought is…	My thinking error or errors are…
My obsessive thought is…	My thinking error or errors are…
My obsessive thought is…	My thinking error or errors are…
My obsessive thought is…	My thinking error or errors are…
My obsessive thought is…	My thinking error or errors are…
My obsessive thought is…	My thinking error or errors are…

Compulsions to Capture

My compulsion is…	My thinking error or errors are…
My compulsion is…	My thinking error or errors are…
My compulsion is…	My thinking error or errors are…
My compulsion is…	My thinking error or errors are…
My compulsion is…	My thinking error or errors are…
My compulsion is…	My thinking error or errors are…
My compulsion is…	My thinking error or errors are…
My compulsion is…	My thinking error or errors are…

CHARLES THOMPSON

Compulsions to Capture

My compulsion is...	My thinking error or errors are...
My compulsion is...	My thinking error or errors are...
My compulsion is...	My thinking error or errors are...
My compulsion is...	My thinking error or errors are...
My compulsion is...	My thinking error or errors are...
My compulsion is...	My thinking error or errors are...
My compulsion is...	My thinking error or errors are...
My compulsion is...	My thinking error or errors are...

All the hard work that you did will be used later as we progress through this workbook together. I want to commend you for not letting fear stop you from inheriting your promised land of freedom from OCD.

You are currently being a Joshua or Caleb!

Have I not commanded you? Be strong and courageous. Do not be afraid; do not be discouraged, for the Lord your God will be with you wherever you go. Joshua 1:9

God and you conquered some territory today that obsessive compulsive disorder was holding.

CHAPTER 10

A Truth Journal

WHERE DO YOU start? Imagine with me that I blindfolded you and drove you out into the middle of a desert that you were not familiar with. Once we stopped, I turned off the car and took off your blindfold. I looked at you and said, "Take us back to where we started". Impossible! You have no clue.

This is how I felt when I began the scientific part of facing and overcoming obsessive compulsive disorder. It felt huge! I did not know where to start. There were too many things I needed to work on.

This is where God gave me an idea. We are going to call it a truth journal. I also think it is something you can start to do that includes the importance of cognitive therapy and exposure.

It is simple.

The premise of doing this can be found in a passage of Scripture.

Then you will know the truth, and the truth will set you free. John 8:32

Now, let's create a sample of a journal page.

Trigger

Obsession Explained

Type or Types of Error Thinking

The Truth to Replace the Obsessive Thought With

Encouraging Verse

I will show you a random example on the next page.

Tape a Dollar Here

Obsession:

My Obsession is that money carries germs and that it is contaminated. I cannot touch it due to this as it could make others or myself sick. If I do touch it, I want to wash my hands. The items it may have touched feel contaminated to me. I also want to avoid places where money is due to the obsession.

Type or Types of Error Thinking:

Overestimating the Probability of Risk
Inability to Tolerate Anxiety or Discomfort

The Truth:

The truth is that I am worried about something that bothers no one else. It has never made me or anyone else sick to handle money.

Avoidance of places where money is has not added to my life, but only taken away from it. Money is in too many places to avoid.

Washing my hands or things that money may have touched is only a compulsion and no one else does it. It is silly.

Verse:

I can do all this through him who gives me strength. Philippians 4:13

My OCD was different than the example above, as my focused on avoidance or getting rid of things that were triggers. I would write a word or saying that was the trigger and then follow the same example.

I did 30 minutes and looked at each page for a period of time using a timer to stay on track. I did it every other day to give myself a break from the exposure periods. You can create your cycle of doing it. All I know is that it helped me and I experienced less anxiety. Do as many triggers in the journal as you can as it helps with obsessive compulsive disorder overall.

You will need to know the type of error thinking from Dr. John Arden[12] in the previous chapter to be able to write at least two or three. Here they are for a short review. If you need the definitions, then look it up.

Either or Thinking

Overestimating the Probability of Risk

Catastrophizing or Overestimating the Severity of Risk

Emotional Reasoning

Overgeneralizing

Superstitious Thinking

Need for Certainty or Persistent Doubting

Excessive Responsibility

Overvalued Thoughts

Thought-Action Fusion

Perfectionism

Inability to Tolerate Anxiety or Discomfort

Focusing on the Negative

Predicting the Future

CHAPTER 11

Heal Your OCD Method

I WANT TO SHARE with you one of the methods that has been very helpful to me, from a secular perspective, that God used in my recovery. It is out of a book called, <u>The Heal Your OCD Workbook: New Techniques to Improve Your Daily Life and Take Back Your Peace of Mind</u> by Ph.D. John Arden and Psy.D. Daniel Dal Corso. The update of this workbook is called <u>Brain Based Therapy for OCD: A Workbook for Clinicians and Clients</u> by Ph. D. John Arden.

I reviewed and used many different books while seeking help, and this one is excellent. I would even recommend you getting a copy for yourself in addition to the Christian workbook that you are holding in your hands. I am thankful that he gave permission to use his resources.

We have to get down to some nuts and bolts here as we start this method of dealing with obsessive compulsive disorder.

ERP – Exposure Response Prevention: This is the practice of someone exposing themselves to what causes anxiety or could be considered a trigger. As time passes through repetition, the anxiety lessens and becomes very manageable.

An example of this would be someone who considers a door handle of a restroom as a trigger that causes anxiety. The exposure could start by being near it. It could progress by touching it. The person would resist washing their hands as it breaks the back of the anxiety. Doing this over and over would get the person eventually to the place it does not bother them to touch a bathroom door handle.

My OCD involved the desire to avoid people, places, or things to prevent anxiety. As part of my exposure, I had to choose to expose myself to those people, places, or things. I got creative and even wrote them in a notebook and exposed myself to the word if I could not go. It was an excellent starting place for me.

Trigger, Situation, or Image – This is something that ignites anxiety related to an obsession and the need to perform a compulsion to get rid of the anxiety.

Obsessive Thought – This is the unwanted thought that comes up and results in anxiety.

SUD – This is simply noticing the level of your anxiety as one being the lowest and one hundred being the highest. It is helpful to sometimes record this and see that it is decreasing as you do exposure.

Thinking Error – You need to identify which thinking errors from the list of fourteen or more are hindering you from getting past the obsession and the compulsion. The truth about the issue needs to be written and understood. The truth is what sets us free!

Compulsive Action – This is the action that you take to relieve the anxiety whether it is rational or not.

Exposure Rules – This is the choice of how you will expose yourself to the trigger, situation, or image.

Response Prevention Rules – This is how you will uniquely handle the exposure to prevent acting on any compulsion or at least limit it.

The following chart is going to be what you do by faith over and over just as the children of Israel took step by step into the Promised Land.

Trigger, Situation, or Image	Obsessive Thought	SUD	Thinking Error	Compulsive Action	Exposure Rules	Response Prevention Rules

We probably need to show a sample of this chart being used for you to be able to use it yourself.

Trigger, Situation, or Image	Obsessive Thought	SUD	Thinking Error	Compulsive Action	Exposure Rules	Response Prevention Rules
Getting my cash drawer at the office and handling the money	Money is filthy. I will be contaminated if it touches my skin.	85	**Overestimating the severity of the risk** – The truth is that money will not contaminate me. **Inability to tolerate anxiety or discomfort** – It has never helped me get better by avoiding it.	I usually wear gloves all day while handling money	I will take a dollar and rub it on my skin an hour before going to work.	I will not wash it off where I rubbed it or change clothes when I get home.

The ERP must increase and change as one thing is conquered by having less or no anxiety by repeating the process. Getting a victory under your belt helps build confidence in furthering the ERP.

Let's say that the person was able to do the above and needed to move on to another step in conquering the fear of money being filthy. Their next chart could look like this.

Trigger, Situation, or Image	Obsessive Thought	SUD	Thinking Error	Compulsive Action	Exposure Rules	Response Prevention Rules
Getting my cash drawer at the office and handling the money	Money is filthy. I will be contaminated if it touches my skin.	50	**Overestimating the severity of the risk** – The truth is that money will not contaminate me. **Inability to tolerate anxiety or discomfort** – It has never helped me get better by avoiding it.	I usually wear gloves all day while handling money	I will not wear gloves after lunch	I will not wash my hands or change my clothes when I get home

This charting process would be repeated over and over as one is completed and a new one is made to increase exposure. The person with OCD will start to notice differences, not just in that one area but other areas that they have obsessive thoughts or compulsions.

I would also encourage any believer doing exposure to involve God by asking for His help, and then maybe having a verse to encourage oneself. *I can do all things through Christ who strengthens me* is a helpful one.

The amount of exposure is dependent on the person and his or her lifestyle. The more you can do, the more you will improve. I would encourage a break between sessions. You did not get into the current obsessive compulsive disorder situation overnight and you will not get out in one exposure unless God intervenes.

The key is in doing something to get better instead of doing nothing.

It is now your turn! We need to start creating a chart for you to do some exposure.

Ask for God's wisdom as you prepare this one as a practice…

If any of you lacks wisdom, you should ask God, who gives generously to all without finding fault, and it will be given to you. James 1:5

Trigger, Situation, or Image	Obsessive Thought	SUD	Thinking Error	Compulsive Action	Exposure Rules	Response Prevention Rules

This is the format you can use over and over as needed to start to inherit your promised land of improved OCD.

I will include two more for you to finalize and start your exposure experience. It may be helpful to get a notebook and create the chart since you will be using one regularly, until you feel you have achieved your desired goal.

Trigger, Situation, or Image	Obsessive Thought	SUD	Thinking Error	Compulsive Action	Exposure Rules	Response Prevention Rules

Trigger, Situation, or Image	Obsessive Thought	SUD	Thinking Error	Compulsive Action	Exposure Rules	Response Prevention Rules

I also want to share a little more from the authors of the <u>Heal Your</u> <u>OCD Workbook</u> in case there is a need for more clarity on their method.

"OCD is psychiatric. That means the brain is not functioning properly. We want to help you get your life back in good, healthy, comfortable working conditions. To do so, your brain needs to be rewired so it is no longer disordered. We created an acronym to help you remember the steps to take when you're having trouble. The acronym is ORDER-ABC."[13]

"**O:** Observe instead of trying to push obsessive thoughts out of your awareness, or neutralize them with compulsive behaviors. You are going to develop your ability to watch your thoughts in doing this. You will become mindful of what you are thinking, and will learn to see obsessive thoughts for what they are: thoughts that you don't like or want flooding your conscience awareness. By increasing your ability to observe your thoughts, you will help yourself detach from your OCD pattern, as if you were just an observer of it, instead of someone feeling the pain.

R: Remind yourself that the thoughts you are having are obsessive compulsive disorder, and you will engage parts of your brain that know OCD is not the real you. You will remind yourself that your brain is not thinking clearly, that the striatum's gate is stuck open, and that the flood of obsessive thoughts and compulsive behaviors is a problem you are working to fix. Reminding pulls the cover off the obsessive compulsive disorder thoughts and keeps you aware of what they are.

D: Do something different than your usual OCD compulsive behaviors, as it helps extinguish the old wiring. The absolute best thing to do is described by the next two letters of our acronym.

E: Exposure is the "E" of the ERP technique that you have learned in this chapter. This involves confronting the situations, thoughts, and images that provoke your OCD. We'll teach you how to do this in a controlled, gradual, step-by-step fashion.

R: Response prevention means refraining from compulsive behaviors that seem to make you feel better but in reality keep you locked into obsessive compulsive disorder. We'll help you make a specific plan involving this key technique to breakout of OCD.

ABC: Allow your brain to change! These steps above are what you need to do to set up the conditions for your brain to do what it wants to do, rewire itself in a way that leads to healthy, optimal functioning."[14]

I would personally like to share with you something else as you follow the method that these wonderful authors present that has been helpful to me. This is a marathon, not a sprint. This is a journey that you are on in getting better when it comes to having OCD. With all that said, show yourself some grace as God shows you grace. You will win some and lose some, but at least you are gaining momentum in changing.

CHAPTER 12

Unlock Your Brain Method

T HERE IS ALSO another doctor and resource that was very helpful to me. His name is Jeffrey M. Schwartz, who discovered breakthrough research that has been very helpful to many. I am thankful to him for the cooperation to make the resources from <u>Brain Lock: Free Yourself from Obsessive Compulsive Disorder</u> available to you in this work.

First, he tells a true story about Howard Hughes that I still go back to when I feel like I do not want to fight against OCD. Let us admit it, we can get tired. The story reminds me to stand up and fight and not grow weary.

"Howard Hughes was dining with actress Jane Greer at Ciro's on the Sunset Strip in Los Angeles one evening in 1947. At one point in the meal, he excused himself to go to the restroom. To Greer's amazement, he did not return for an hour and a half. When he finally reappeared, she was astonished to see that he was soaking wet from head to toe. 'What on earth happened to you?' she asked. 'Well,' Hughes said, 'I spilled some catsup on my shirt and pants and had to wash them out in the sink.' He then let them dry for a while, hanging them over one of the toilet stalls. Once he put his clothes back on, he explained, 'I couldn't leave the restroom because I couldn't touch the door handle. I had to wait for someone to come in.' According to Peter H. Brown, coauthor with Pat Broeske of Howard Hughes: <u>The</u> <u>Untold Story</u>, Jane Greer never went out with Hughes again.

Howard Hughes was eccentric, certainly, but he was not a freak. He was suffering from obsessive compulsive disorder (OCD), a classic and severe case. By the end of his life, in 1976, he was overwhelmed by the disease. He spent his last days in isolation in his top floor suite at the Princess Hotel in Acapulco, where he had sealed himself in a hospital like atmosphere, terrified of germs. Blackout curtains at every window kept all sunlight out; the sun, he thought, might transmit germs he so dreaded. Aides with facial tissues covering their hands brought him food, which had to be precisely cut and measured.

Sadly, there was no treatment for OCD in Howard Hughes' lifetime. It would be another decade before the disease would be identified as a brain-related disorder.

I frequently cite the case of Howard Hughes to help patients understand that this disease, obsessive compulsive disorder, is an insatiable monster. The more you give in, the hungrier it gets. Even Hughes, with all his millions – and a retinue of servants to perform the bizarre rituals his OCD told him to perform – could not buy his way out. Eventually, the false messages coming from his brain overwhelmed him.

OCD is a tenacious enemy, but a strong-willed, motivated person can overcome it."[15]

1. *What did you learn from the story of Howard Hughes?*

2. *How does his story encourage you to fight instead of giving in to obsessive compulsive disorder?*

As we go into battle to take our promised land as Joshua and Caleb did, we have to remember the words spoken by the Apostle Paul.

Let us not become weary in doing good, for at the proper time we will reap a harvest if we do not give up. Galatians 6:9

1. *How does obsessive compulsive disorder make you weary sometimes?*

2. *How can you not grow weary in well doing in the commitment to get better with obsessive compulsive disorder?*

3. *What can happen if we do not grow weary and stay firm in facing our fears with God's help?*

One of the next things that stood out to me by Dr. Jeffrey M. Schwartz is the PET scan that has been done on people with OCD. I would like to share with you a copy of one of the photos from his research below.[16]

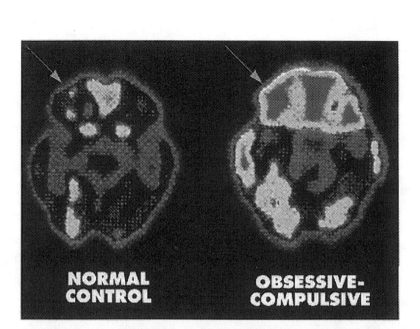

NORMAL CONTROL   **OBSESSIVE-COMPULSIVE**

HIGH ENERGY USE IN THE BRAIN OF A TYPICAL PERSON WITH OCD

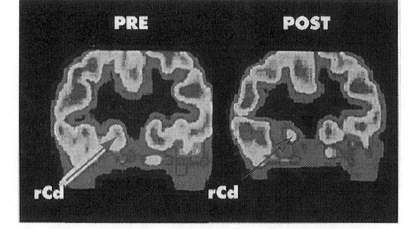

PRE   **POST**

rCd   rCd

CHANGE IN ENERGY USE AFTER DRUG-FREE SELF-TREATMENT WITH FOUR-STEP METHOD

The brain on the left is that of a person without OCD and the one on the right is that of a person with OCD. The images are as different as day and night. The person with obsessive compulsive disorder uses a considerable more energy on a regular basis in the orbital cortez found on the underside of the brain. It is working overtime to try to deal with the disorder and is heating up. This amount of energy has also been shown to decrease when treated with exposure and proven techniques such as found in the methods section of this workbook.

The picture is proof that obsessive compulsive disorder is a brain disorder. Once people understand the nature of OCD, they are better armed to carry out the behavior therapy that leads to recovery. The culprit is the neurological imbalance in the brain. Just knowing, "It's not me – it's my OCD" is a stress reliever itself that enables the focus to get better.[17]

1. *What is your reaction to the fact that your OCD brain looks different than a normal person's brain?*

2. *How does it help you to know there is proof that obsessive compulsive disorder is a chemical imbalance?*

3. *How can it help you to face your obsessions and compulsions by saying, "It's not me – it's my OCD"?*

A story that Dr. Jeffrey wrote helped me to realize I was not the only Christian to deal with OCD. It is reported that John Bunyan, who lived in the seventeenth century, had religious obsessive compulsive disorder. He was a minister who wrote Pilgrim's Progress. He agonized over his irreverent thoughts. He eventually came to the place that he believed God would be upset with him if he punished himself for having false and meaningless thoughts. He did not know all we do today about OCD, but it sure helps us understand that God is able to separate us from our obsessions and compulsions.[18]

1. How can the reality that John Bunyan came to help you?

2. How is God able to separate OCD from our true identity?

There is also a Christian mentioned in the book that found comfort in a passage of Scripture that we can also use when dealing with obsessive compulsive disorder. *"A deeply religious man, Chet also turned to the Scriptures for inspiration and found comfort in the passage "The Lord searcheth all hearts and He understands all the imaginations of the mind",* (1 Chronicles 28:9). Chet clearly understood how this passage applied to him: God understands my heart and knows that my mind is messed up. I must work to stop beating myself up over it."[19]

1. How can the passage that encouraged Chet encourage you?

2. *How can Chet's statement help you in your Christian walk with obsessive compulsive disorder?*

We are now going to address the final component that includes the method that Jeffrey M. Scwartz M.D. uses to help people.

4 Steps to Take

1. **RELABLE** – Relabel means calling the intrusive unwanted thoughts and behaviors what they really are: obsessions and compulsions. Relabeling will not take them away immediately, but it will prepare you to change your behavioral responses. When you change your behavior, you change your brain.[20]

   A. *What is the relabel step in your own words?*

   B. *How can you start using it in your day to day reality with obsessive compulsive disorder?*

2. **REATTRIBUTE** – Reattribute means answering the questions, "Why do these thoughts and urges keep bothering me? Why don't they go away?" The answer is, because of a medical conditional called OCD. obsessive compulsive disorder is related to a biochemical imbalance in the brain that results in a

malfunction of the brain's gearshift: the brain gets stuck in gear! Because the brain is stuck in gear, its error detection circuit keeps firing inappropriately. This causes very uncomfortable feelings. Changing your behavioral responses to the uncomfortable feelings and shifting to useful and constructive behaviors will, over time, make the broken gearshift come unstuck.[21]

A. What is the reattribute step in your own words?

B. How can you apply the reattribute step to your daily routine of overcoming OCD?

3. **REFOCUS** – Refocus means to change your behavioral responses to unwanted thoughts and urges and focus your attention on something useful and constructive. Do another behavior! This is the no pain, no gain step. You must be active. You cannot be passive. Use the fifteen minute rule: Work around your symptoms by doing something wholesome and enjoyable for at least fifteen minutes. After fifteen minutes, make mental notes of how your symptoms have changed and try to refocus for another fifteen minutes.[22]

A. What is the refocus step in your own words?

B. *How can you do the refocus step in dealing with obsessive compulsive disorder in daily living?*

4. **REVALUE** – Revalue means don't take your symptoms at face value as they do not mean what they say. See them for what they are. Work to revalue in an active way, by seeing the reality of the situation as quickly and clearly as possible. Strengthen the clarity of your observation with assertive mental notes such as, "It's not me – it's just OCD." When you revalue and devalue unwanted thoughts and urges, you are strengthening your Impartial Spectator and building a powerful mind. A mind that can take note of subtle changes and understand the implications of those changes is a powerful mind. A powerful mind can change the brain by altering responses to the messages the brain sends. This is true self-command. It results in self-esteem.[23]

A. *What does it mean to revalue in your own words?*

B. *How can you revalue day to day in your battle with OCD?*

CHAPTER 13

Truth

DURING 2015 I had the opportunity to take part in the <u>Transformed: How God Changes Us</u> series done by Rick Warren and greatly benefited from it. The workbook you have in your hands was thought of and cultivated by God due to the impact of one session encouraging us to allow the Lord to use what we have been through in life to help others.

Rick Warren understands the factors of mental health issues due to having firsthand experience and also approaches it in a mercifully Biblical way. There is no way that I can explain the mental health section in his work in a word for word format, but in this chapter it is my goal to summarize what can be helpful for Christians with OCD. If you would like to go through the whole Transformation series, it covers spiritual, physical, mental, emotional, relational, financial, and vocational health. You can purchase the video and the workbook to let God mold you. My summary is in no way a substitute.

Rick explains in the parts applicable to us that there are five keys to mental health. An acrostic is used called THINK.[24] Then after going through the acrostic, I have created some unrelated devotionals for you to go through for five days to learn how to spend some time with God.

Test every thought. Do not believe everything that you think.

Obsessions and compulsions are all about thoughts. The obsession is an unwanted thought and the compulsion is an unwanted action. Half of the battle, when it comes to obsessive compulsive disorder, is the ability to control the obsessions and compulsions instead of letting them be in control of you. If you let the obsessive and compulsive thoughts be in control, there is one thing for certain: anxiety will abound!

Testing a thought is Biblical.

Philippians 4:8 says, *Finally, brothers and sisters, whatever is true...... think about such things.*

1. *How can we test a thought according to this passage?*

2. *How can you use truth to test your obsessions?*

3. *How can you use truth to test your compulsions?*

4. *If an obsession tells you that you just ran someone over with the car, what is the truth?*

5. *If a compulsion tells you to go back and check to see if you ran someone over, what is the truth?*

This can apply to checking doors, washing hands due to a fear of germs, using knives, cleaning the home, showering, hoarding, and much more.

There are some other areas to think about truth in regards to the spiritual aspect of dealing with OCD.

God, the Holy Spirit, is called the Spirit of truth. He lives in you and can give you wisdom about your obsessions and compulsions. He can cut through your raw emotions and let you know that they are to be disregarded. You might just ask God, "What is the truth about this?"

We have also been given the Bible as truth. It is our guide for moral living and wise decision making. You can apply a truth of scripture to your obsessions or compulsions.

Testing a thought can lead to interrupting the obsessive or compulsive thoughts and avoiding carrying them out.

Helmet your head! Guard your mind against garbage like negativity.

The mind is a powerful thing. It is profound that you can go a lifetime and never run out of space in that thing called the brain. Computers get outdated, but the mind does not.

Finally, brothers and sisters, whatever is ....noble,....pure....excellent or praiseworthy—think about such things. Philippians 4:8

1. ***What type of things do we need to fill our mind with according to this verse?***

The things listed are all positive things. A person with obsessive compulsive disorder does not need any help coming up with something negative, as the disorder does it, and then he or she can feel downcast.

You need to protect your head.

2. How can you fill it full of positive things daily?

3. How can you position yourself around positive people?

4. How can you change your negative talk to positive?

The allowance of negativity is like fuel to the fire for obsessive compulsive disorder, or like a slip in the snow that causes an avalanche.

Imagine great thoughts. Let God stretch your imagination and dream big with Him due to the great plan He has for you.

OCD can seem like it has a chokehold and it drains the life out of you for daily living. It can feel like a dream killer.

For I know the plans I have for you, declares the Lord, plans to prosper you and not to harm you, plans to give you hope and a future. Jeremiah 29:11

1. What type of plan does God have for your life according to Jeremiah 29:11?

It is time for you to throw the restraints of obsessive compulsive disorder off, and not let it decide what you do or do not do. You are going to miss out on so much life that God wants for you to experience if you do not start dreaming again.

2.   *What dream do you have for your life?*

3.   *In what way is OCD in the way of it?*

4.   *What can you do with God's help to take a step of faith and start to fulfill that dream?*

5.   *What type of things has OCD stopped you from enjoying?*

6.   *What are the truths that can help you start to do those enjoyable things again, even if it is little by little?*

Nourish a godly mind. Renew your mind in the Word of God and prayer on a daily basis.

The treatment for OCD without Jesus is meaningless. Jesus is the center. An ongoing relationship with God will give you the strength, wisdom, help, hope, and fulfillment to face the disorder over and over.

As the deer pants for streams of water, so my soul pants for you, my God. Psalms 42:1

1. What type of relationship with God does the Psalmist describe here?

A relationship with God needs what we call a devotional time, as part of it. You can pick the time, the place, and the reading in the Bible. The key is to do this daily and pick it back up if you miss a day as God is not mad at you. He missed you!

2. What is the best time for you to have a devotional time with God?

3. Where will you set aside a quiet place to do this daily?

You might get a notebook and a pen. Pray before you start and be expectant to hear from God. Underline in your Bible what verse or verses stand out to you. When you are done reading whatever amount you desire, write the verse that stood out, what it means to you, and what you are going to do about it.

Prayer should also be a part of a devotional time. It is merely talking to God. Tell him about what you just read, what is on your mind, ask for help, pray for others, and do not forget to make time to listen to God when you ask things. He will speak.

A tool is provided for you to use the next five days in this chapter to spend time with God.

Keep on learning. Do not become stagnant by thinking you have arrived. Keep humble and keep learning.

Blessed are those who find wisdom, those who gain understanding. Proverbs 3:13

I have found that there are times that I need to step back and review what OCD is and what to do about it. You would think after all these years this would not be necessary. It is absolutely necessary.

1. *What does the verse above say?*

In its original context it is talking about being a lifelong learner of the Word of God. Trust me, being a lifelong learner of God is a blessing.

I also think there is blessing in finding wisdom about obsessive compulsive disorder. There is help in understanding OCD.

I would advise you to learn, learn, learn, and learn about the disorder.

When obsessions and compulsions seem to be getting the best of me due to their powerful influence over the emotions, I go back and look at what is happening, and why, from a scientific perspective. It helps me gain perspective in the midst of fear.

1. *Why do you think you need to be a lifelong learner about obsessive compulsive disorder?*

2. *How do you think being a lifelong learner about OCD can be helpful?*

I would note one caution here in your learning; let what you always learn be compared to the Bible as our relationship with God, for living by His commands is paramount.

Day 1

And we know that in all things God works for the good of those who love him, who have been called according to his purpose. Romans 8:28

What stood out to you about this verse?

How can you apply this verse to your life right now?

Day 2

*What, then, shall we say in response to these things? If God is for us, who can be against us? He who did not spare his own Son, but gave him up for us all—how will he not also, along with him, graciously give us all things.*Romans 8:31-32

What stood out to you about these verses?

How can you apply these verses to your life right now?

Day 3

Who will bring any charge against those whom God has chosen? It is God who justifies. Who then is the one who condemns? No one. Christ Jesus who died—more than that, who was raised to life—is at the right hand of God and is also interceding for us. Romans 8:33-34

What stood out to you about these verses?

How can you apply these verses to your life right now?

Day 4

For I am convinced that neither death nor life, neither angels nor demons, neither the present nor the future, nor any powers, neither height nor depth, nor anything else in all creation, will be able to separate us from the love of God that is in Christ Jesus our Lord. Romans 8:38-39

What stood out to you about these verses?

How can you apply these verses to your life right now?

Day 5

Therefore, there is now no condemnation for those who are in Christ Jesus. Romans 8:1

What stood out to you about this verse?

How can you apply this verse to your life right now?

CHAPTER 14

Motivation to Change

G OD LOOKS AT your heart. We know this because of the words that were spoken to Samuel in the Bible when he was choosing a new king.

...The Lord does not look at the things people look at. People look at the outward appearance, but the Lord looks at the heart. 1 Samuel 16:7b

This passage of Scripture should cause anyone with obsessive compulsive disorder to rejoice in who God is and the way that He sees you. In the midst of all the unwanted obsessions and compulsions, it is possible to take them so personally that we can feel God is disappointed in us. We may feel dirty.

1.   How does OCD make you feel sometimes about yourself?

God is able to magnificently separate us from our OCD. He sees our real heart. He knows we want the thoughts gone. He knows we are not that type of person. He sees us as clean by what His One and only Son did for us. God grasps that the thoughts and compulsions are caused by a chemical imbalance.

1.   How does it make you feel to know God is able to separate the two?

Does that mean we are totally off the hook? I think there is an area that we do have choice in that needs to be explored. The obsessions and compulsions are there and we do not want them, but we do have a choice about what we do with them.

One of our dogs is a little Chihuahua named Shadow. He is the alpha male who thinks he is the leader of the pack. Did I mention he is smaller than the other two dogs? It does not stop him. Lacy and Peanut are Chi-weenies. If they receive a dog treat or some human food, they eat it like they have not had anything for weeks. They inhale it. Shadow is a different story. He will take his and sit it in front of him. He will watch for Lacy and Peanut and growl at them. He will not enjoy it, but instead tries to protect it. It is funny; sometimes they sneak it away from him. I deep down just wish he would eat it. It does not need to be guarded for thirty minutes. When I put new dog food in the two bowls, it becomes a competition for the alpha dog. He will growl like he is going to take the other dogs out. He will throw himself in the bowl literally. He will throw dog food all over the floor and around the bowl. Water will be splashed around. Man! It is a mess to clean up. If I was to find one word to describe the actions above it would be selfish.

SELFISH...

OCD can make us selfish. We can get so wrapped up into the world of obsessions and compulsions, that we are distracted. We miss out on opportunities to build relationships and memories. Our service to God, family, and friends is not the priority it could be. The time consumed cannot be retrieved.

Be very careful, then, how you live—not as unwise but as wise, making the most of every opportunity.... Ephesians 5:15-16a

1. *What does this passage say about using our time?*

2. Is it wise to use our time and not be consumed with obsessions?

3. Is it wise to use our time and not be consumed with compulsions?

It is our choice to give control to obsessions or compulsions. They are resistible and there is a way out. We have to do the hard work of taking back control and not allowing obsessive compulsive disorder to waste our life.

I am not saying that you will be perfect and never have issues with obsessions and compulsions. There will be battles won and there will be battles lost. The point is not to let OCD win the war.

You have to step out in faith and choose to spend time with family.

You have to choose to step out in faith and do something with other people.

You have to choose to step out in faith and develop friendships.

You have to choose to step out in faith and go do something you enjoy.

You have to choose to step out in faith and go to church.

You have to choose to step out in faith and spend time with God personally in the Bible and prayer.

You have to choose to step out in faith and do something for God using your spiritual gifts and talents.

1. *How have your obsessions robbed you of time that could have been given to these things above?*

2. *How have compulsions robbed your of time that could have been given to these things above?*

3. *What actions can you take to get back what you have been missing?*

The Motivation to Change for God

28 One of the teachers of the law came and heard them debating. Noticing that Jesus had given them a good answer, he asked him, "Of all the commandments, which is the most important?" 29 The most important one," answered Jesus, "is this: 'Hear, O Israel: The Lord our God, the Lord is one. 30 Love the Lord your God with all your heart and with all your soul and with all your mind and with all your strength.' 31 The second is this: 'Love your neighbor as yourself. Mark 12:28-31

1. *What did the teacher of the law ask Jesus in Mark 12:28?*

2. What was important to Jesus according to Mark 12:30?

3. What was next in importance to Jesus according to Mark 12:31?

This is God's will for our life as these sum up the whole Bible. If a believer does or does not have OCD, they are always the priority.

The choice must be made on a regular basis to move from selfishness in allowing OCD to be in control and for us say no! I will choose to be a servant by loving God and others. Love is an action.

I do not want to look back on life and see that there were so many missed opportunities that I could have taken advantage of because I chose not to fight obsessive compulsive disorder, and let anxiety prevent me from doing things.

Sleep must not be allowed to be in control to escape obsessions and compulsions either. Anxiety can make you tired. It is wise to take care of yourself and give breaks, but not to isolate away from everybody and everything.

1. How can you give yourself a break sometimes?

2. *Why is giving yourself a break important?*

3. *How much of a break would be considered balanced?*

4. *What would be considered out of balance for a break?*

Interaction improves the quality of life for someone with OCD. Inherit your promised land and do not let fear prevent you from laughing and enjoying life.

Let me be transparent here. I have a call on my life to be in ministry. The interesting thing is that part of my obsessive compulsive disorder is religious oriented. I have to make the choice on a regular basis to fulfill the call on my life despite obsessions and compulsions. I have found and always will, that the benefit of not letting OCD be in control, brings fulfillment when doing what Jesus made me to be and do.

What do you enjoy? I think it is time to do it.

CHAPTER 15

Celebrate Recovery and OCD

M ILLIONS OF PEOPLE around the United States and the world have benefited from a Christian program called Celebrate Recovery. I have personally read the curriculum and felt that it was helpful to me. I also feel that it may be helpful to you in overcoming obsessive compulsive disorder. This belief has led me to include them in Jesus and OCD Workbook with adaptations to apply to the disorder specifically. So, the rest of this chapter will be turned into a Bible study to bring additional freedom to what you have already experienced to this point. This is only a small part of Celebrate Recovery and for further help you can find a local group that meets and join. Please tell the leader of the group you are there to find help with OCD.

Principle 1[25]

Realize I'm not God, I admit that I am powerless to control my tendency to do the wrong thing and that my life is unmanageable.

Let's look at Nehemiah to start to implement this principle.

The words of Nehemiah son of Hakaliah: In the month of Kislev in the twentieth year, while I was in the citadel of Susa, Hanani, one of my brothers, came from Judah with some other men, and I questioned them about the Jewish remnant that had survived the exile, and also about Jerusalem. They said to me, "Those who survived the exile and are back in the province are in great trouble and disgrace. The wall of Jerusalem is broken down, and its gates have been burned with fire." When I heard these things, I sat down and wept. For some days I mourned and fasted and prayed before the God of heaven. Nehemiah 1:1-4

1. **What did Nehemiah learn about the Jewish remnant and Jerusalem?**

2. **What was Nehemiah's response to this news?**

Nehemiah knew that he could not do one thing as a mere servant of the king, to change the fact the people of Jerusalem were in great trouble, and had no city walls to protect them.

He knew that God was the only one who could do something in this out of control circumstance. When it comes to OCD you must realize that you are in great trouble and you have no city walls to protect you. You cannot get out of the great trouble by yourself.

3. **How can you do what Nehemiah did?**

Principle 2

Earnestly believe that God exists, that I matter to Him, and that He has the power to help me recover.

OCD can make a person feel alone and isolated. The questions can come like, "Does anyone care about me?" or "Does God care about me?" The question about God must be settled to receive help from Him.

Therefore I tell you, do not worry about your life, what you will eat or drink; or about your body, what you will wear. Is not life more than food, and the body more than clothes? Look at the birds of the air; they do not sow or reap or store away in barns, and yet your heavenly Father feeds them. Are you not much more valuable than they? Can any one of you by worrying add a single hour to your life? "And why do you worry about clothes? See how the flowers of the field grow. They do not labor or spin. Yet I tell you that not even Solomon in all his splendor was dressed like one of these. If that is how God clothes the grass of the field, which is here today and tomorrow is thrown into the fire, will he not much more clothe you—you of little faith? So do not worry, saying, 'What shall we eat?' or 'What shall we drink?' or 'What shall we wear?' For the pagans run after all these things, and your heavenly Father knows that you need them. But seek first his kingdom and his righteousness, and all these things will be given to you as well. Therefore do not worry about tomorrow, for tomorrow will worry about itself. Each day has enough trouble of its own. Matthew 6:25-34

1. What does this passage say about the personal care God has for you?

2. How does the realization God cares about you help face obsessive compulsive disorder?

Principle 3

Consciously choose to commit all my life and will to Christ's care and control.

Trust in the Lord with all your heart and lean not on your own understanding; in all your ways submit to him, and he will make your paths straight. Proverbs 3:5-6

OCD is all about control. You want to be in control of the obsessions. How has your attempt worked? You want to be in control of the compulsions. How has your attempt worked? There is absolutely no way to be in control of everything to make sure you never have a thought or trigger.

You must reach a point of surrender in which you let go and let God. Give Him the control when you face an obsession or compulsion. Learn to handle it as He would and trust Him.

1. *How does Proverbs 3:5-6 encourage us to give up control and turn it over to God with obsessions and compulsions?*

Principle 4

Openly examine and confess my faults to myself, to God, and someone I trust.

As iron sharpens iron, so one person sharpens another. Proverbs 27:17

We live in a suck it up culture. People are supposed to act like they are fine. They are supposed to keep their troubles to themselves. I have one word for that, "bologna".

The Bible tells us to the do the opposite.

We need to be honest and transparent with God.

1. *How can we do this with OCD?*

2. *Why do we leave God out with OCD sometimes?*

3. *What is the benefit of including Him?*

We need to be honest and transparent with ourselves.

4. *How can we do this with OCD?*

5. *Why do we go into denial with OCD sometimes?*

6. *What is the benefit of being honest with ourselves with this disorder?*

We need to be honest and transparent with others.

7. *How can we do this with OCD?*

8. *Why do we leave trusted others out when it comes to OCD?*

9. *What are the benefits of opening up to others about OCD?*

Principle 5

Voluntarily submit to every change that God wants to make in my life and humbly ask Him to remove my character defects.

Do not merely listen to the word, and so deceive yourselves. Do what it says. Anyone who listens to the word but does not do what it says is like someone who looks at his face in a mirror and, after looking at himself, goes away and immediately forgets what he looks like. But whoever looks intently into the perfect law that gives freedom, and continues in it—not forgetting what they have heard, but doing it—they will be blessed in what they do. James 1:23-25

Do you want to get better? There is a clear cut thing you must do if you want to get better. If you do not do this one thing, you will stay as you are.

It is absolutely to do whatever God tells you to do as you are working on inheriting your promised land and overcoming OCD.

It is also important to follow the advice of your health professionals and do the work found in this workbook to overcome obsessive compulsive disorder.

1. *Why is action needed to do what God tells you to do when it comes to obsessive compulsive disorder?*

2. **Why is it important to do what your healthcare professionals say, as well as the lessons learned in this workbook?**

Action equals improvement!

Principle 6

Evaluate all my relationships. Offer forgiveness to those who have hurt me and make amends to harm I have done to others, except when to do so would hurt them or others.

This has been covered to a large extent in Chapter 4. If you feel it still needs to be addressed, please go back and do that section again.

If we choose to not give forgiveness to others who have hurt us, then anger, bitterness, and desire for revenge are sure to follow. Stress will then be following us around, and it only increases OCD symptoms.

> 1. *Why do you think forgiveness is important to the improvement of OCD?*

Principle 7

Reserve a daily time with God for self-examination, bible reading and prayer in order to know God, His will for my life, and to gain the power to follow His will.

We also discussed this important principle previously in Chapter 13.

I am the vine; you are the branches. If you remain in me and I in you, you will bear much fruit; apart from me you can do nothing. John 15:5

Jesus is the vine. You are a branch of that vine.

1. Where does a branch get its nourishment in nature?

2. Where will you get your nourishment to overcome OCD as a Christian?

3. How important is God in bearing fruit to overcome OCD?

Make sure you develop a routine of spending time with God in prayer and the Word.

Principle 8

Yield myself to God to be used to bring this Good News to others, both by my example and by my words.

This is what I am doing with you in this whole Jesus and OCD Workbook. I decided to let God use what I had been through to help others.

You must also eventually choose not to be so secretive about your obsessive compulsive disorder. You will find that there are people around you who need what you have to offer.

The more I have been open, the more people I found around me who also had obsessive compulsive disorder. The more people I knew that had the disorder, presented the opportunity to encourage them and pray for them.

1. *Is there someone with obsessive compulsive disorder that you can start to encourage and pray for?*

CHAPTER 16

Accountability and Prayer Support

I MAGINE WITH ME that you are a soccer goalie and the other team is advancing down the field in an attempt to score a point. To your surprise, you look up and notice that all your offensive and defensive players are taking a break at the water cooler. The opposing team is coming at you and there is no one to help.

1. What would you feel like if you were the goalie?

It surprises me that we can so easily think that the goalie should have had his team there to help him, but we are so willing to go at OCD alone. The disease already makes you feel alone, why contribute to it by being alone, quiet, and never asking for help?

There are people around the water cooler as the example above, but they are oblivious that you need their help on the field of obsessive compulsive disorder. You are alone as the goalie only if you have chosen to play the game that way. God put people around you, and it is time to take advantage of this wonderful resource.

There are many examples in the Bible of this type of support that you need as you face the day to day battles with OCD.

JONATHAN AND DAVID (Love Supports)

And Jonathan made a covenant with David because he loved him as himself. Jonathan took off the robe he was wearing and gave it to David, along with his tunic, and even his sword, his bow and his belt. 1 Samuel 18:3-4

1. ***What did Jonathan make with David?***

2. ***How did Jonathan love David?***

3. ***What did Jonathan give David?***

Jonathan became one of David's closest friends who was with him through thick and thin. It says that a covenant was made and that shows the level of commitment that was established and lived out. Jesus said that we are to love our neighbor as ourselves and that is exactly what Jonathan did in the Old Testament with his friend who would be king of Israel one day. Jonathan also gave of his time and belongings to his close friend.

You need to find someone or a few people on this journey with OCD than can be a Jonathan to you.

Look for someone who is committed to you.

Look for someone who loves you like God does.

Look for someone who will give their time and help to you.

4. *What other traits do you think are important for you to look for in a Jonathan that will be a close friend to you?*

Jonathan had a huge part that he played in protecting and encouraging David on the road to become the king. Whomever you find to be a Jonathan for you, will also play a role of protecting and encouraging on the road to overcoming obsessive compulsive disorder. It will need to be someone with compassion.

5. *Can you think of someone who might be an excellent Jonathan for you?* **Write their name here. Now come up with a plan to ask them.**

If you cannot think of a Jonathan, ask God to help you find one. You could write a prayer out here.

It is possible that you will need to help them understand OCD and even be aware of your unique situation. I am thankful for the Jonathans God has put in my life.

PETER AND PRAYER (Love Prays)

After arresting him, he put him in prison, handing him over to be guarded by four squads of four soldiers each. Herod intended to bring him out for public trial after the Passover. So Peter was kept in prison, but the church was earnestly praying to God for him. The night before Herod was to bring him to trial, Peter was sleeping between two soldiers, bound with two chains, and sentries stood guard at the entrance. 7 Suddenly an angel of the Lord appeared and a light shone in the cell. He struck Peter on the side and woke him up. "Quick, get up!" he said, and the chains fell off Peter's wrists. Then the angel said to him, "Put on your clothes and sandals." And Peter did so. "Wrap your cloak around you and follow me," the angel told him. 9 Peter followed him out of the prison. Acts 12:4-9a

1. **What happened to Peter at the beginning of this passage?**

2. **What was the church doing?**

3. **What was the result?**

I am guessing that the Apostle Peter also prayed as he was in jail, but it was not mentioned. The emphasis is put on the believers gathering in a home and praying with all their heart that he would be released from prison. Their prayers are what made the difference. God sent an angel and led him out of prison! The result of their intercession on Peter's behalf even shocked them when he showed up on the doorstep of where they were praying.

CHARLES THOMPSON

OCD can make you feel like a prisoner. It is important to have some trustworthy people you can call on to pray for you. You can call them! You can email them! You can text them! The method does not matter as much as that you simply do it. Just as the Apostle Peter was set free from prison by prayer, God can set you free from the prison of OCD as others lift you up.

4. *Can you think of some people who may fill that role for you?* **Write their names below.**

The battle with OCD can seem intense. In those times, it is appropriate to call upon your intercessors.

5. *What times with your specific obsessions and compulsions do you think that you need people praying for you?*

While we are on the subject of prayer, I would encourage you to go beyond asking for people to pray for you while you are struggling, to asking personal Christian friends to pray for total healing in your body. This book is about dealing with OCD as a process, but I also believe God is the same yesterday, today, and forever. He healed in the Bible, so He can still do it for you. I also believe you can ask God to heal you. What if I am not healed? I would rather say that I gave God a chance than to never ask. What if this time you ask is the time you are healed? This is not about your great amount for faith for God to answer your friend's prayers or your own. The Bible says faith as small as a mustard seed can move a mountain. The same grace that saved you is the same grace that can heal you.

PAUL AND PETER (Love Confronts)

There will be times that you need accountability in the steps of faith to take your promised land of better obsessive compulsive disorder. It involves someone telling us what we need to hear in love.

When Cephas came to Antioch, I opposed him to his face, because he stood condemned. For before certain men came from James, he used to eat with the Gentiles. But when they arrived, he began to draw back and separate himself from the Gentiles because he was afraid of those who belonged to the circumcision group. The other Jews joined him in his hypocrisy, so that by their hypocrisy even Barnabas was led astray. When I saw that they were not acting in line with the truth of the gospel, I said to Cephas in front of them all, "You are a Jew, yet you live like a Gentile and not like a Jew. How is it, then, that you force Gentiles to follow Jewish customs? "We who are Jews by birth and not sinful Gentiles know that a person is not justified by the works of the law, but by faith in Jesus Christ. So we, too, have put our faith in Christ Jesus that we may be justified by faith in[d] Christ and not by the works of the law, because by the works of the law no one will be justified. Galatians 2:11-16

We would say that Peter was the Apostle to the Jews and that Paul was the Apostle to the Gentiles. Both men had a close relationship with God and were used in mighty ways. Peter was not flawless and neither are we.

1. What was Peter doing?

2. What problem did it cause?

3. *What was Paul's response?*

The Apostle Paul loved Peter enough to tell him the truth that he needed to hear. We need the same when it comes to OCD.

4. *Why do we need someone who is direct when it comes to our obsessions and compulsions?*

5. **What is the benefit of having someone who loves you enough to confront about OCD?**

What Paul did changed Peter's life, and when we have someone intervene or tell the truth about what we need to hear about OCD, it can do the same.

6. *Who is someone you can go to that can be a Paul for you?*

7. *What attitude does it take to hear and act upon the truth told by a Paul?*

NOTES

1 http://beyondocd.org/ocd-facts
2 Schwartz, Jeffrey M. M.D. <u>Brain Lock: Free Yourself from Obsessive Compulsive Behavior,</u> E-Book Published 2009, Harper Collins Publishers, New York, NY 10022.
3 Jeffrey Schwartz
4 Miller-Keane Encyclopedia and Dictionary of Medicine, Nursing, and Allied Health, Seventh Edition. © 2003 by Saunders, an imprint of Elsevier, Inc. All rights reserved.
5 Miller-Keane Encyclopedia and Dictionary of Medicine, Nursing, and Allied Health, Seventh Edition. © 2003 by Saunders, an imprint of Elsevier, Inc. All rights reserved.
6 Miller-Keane Encyclopedia and Dictionary of Medicine, Nursing, and Allied Health, Seventh Edition. © 2003 by Saunders, an imprint of Elsevier, Inc. All rights reserved.
7 Charles Thompson, definition by experience of counseling others myself
8 http://www.webmd.com/drugs/condition-976-Obsessive-Compulsive+ Disorder.aspx?diseaseid=976&diseasename=Obsessive-Compulsive+ Disorder
9 http://www.bjs.gov/index.cfm?ty=tp&tid=42
10 Compiled By Neil Anderson
11 Arden, John Ph.D. and Corso, Daniel Dal Psy.D. The Heal Your OCD Workbook: New Techniques to Improve Your Daily Life and Take Back Your Peace of Mind, Fair Winds Press, Beverly, MA 01915-6101, 2009, Pages 44-46.
12 Arden, John Ph.D. and Corso, Daniel Dal Psy.D. The Heal Your OCD Workbook: New Techniques to Improve Your Daily Life and Take Back Your Peace of Mind, Fair Winds Press, Beverly, MA 01915-6101, 2009, Pages 44-46.
13 Arden, John Ph.D. and Corso, Daniel Dal Psy.D. The Heal Your OCD Workbook: New Techniques to Improve Your Daily Life and Take Back Your Peace of Mind, Fair Winds Press, Beverly, MA 01915-6101, 2009, Page 76.
14 Arden, John Ph.D. and Corso, Daniel Dal Psy.D. The Heal Your OCD Workbook: New Techniques to Improve Your Daily Life and Take Back

Your Peace of Mind, Fair Winds Press, Beverly, MA 01915-6101, 2009, Page 76.

15 Schwartz, Jeffrey M. M.D. Brain Lock: Free Yourself from Obsessive Compulsive Behavior, E-Book Published 2009, Harper Collins Publishers, New York, NY 10022, Introduction.

16 From Brain Lock Twentieth Anniversary Edition by Jeffrey M. Schwartz, MD p. xlvii & p.59

17 Schwartz, Jeffrey M. M.D. Brain Lock: Free Yourself from Obsessive Compulsive Behavior, E-Book Published 2009, Harper Collins Publishers, New York, NY 10022, Introduction.

18 Schwartz, Jeffrey M. M.D. Brain Lock: Free Yourself from Obsessive Compulsive Behavior, E-Book Published 2009, Harper Collins Publishers, New York, NY 10022, Chapter 1.

19 Schwartz, Jeffrey M. M.D. Brain Lock: Free Yourself from Obsessive Compulsive Behavior, E-Book Published 2009, Harper Collins Publishers, New York, NY 10022, Chapter 1.

20 Schwartz, Jeffrey M. M.D. Brain Lock: Free Yourself from Obsessive Compulsive Behavior, E-Book Published 2009, Harper Collins Publishers, New York, NY 10022, Chapter 1.

21 Schwartz, Jeffrey M. M.D. Brain Lock: Free Yourself from Obsessive Compulsive Behavior, E-Book Published 2009, Harper Collins Publishers, New York, NY 10022, Chapter 2.

22 Schwartz, Jeffrey M. M.D. Brain Lock: Free Yourself from Obsessive Compulsive Behavior, E-Book Published 2009, Harper Collins Publishers, New York, NY 10022, Chapter 3.

23 Schwartz, Jeffrey M. M.D. Brain Lock: Free Yourself from Obsessive Compulsive Behavior, E-Book Published 2009, Harper Collins Publishers, New York, NY 10022, Chapter 4.

24 Warren, Rick Transformed: How God Changes Us, Saddleback Church Publishers, Rancho Santa, Margarita, CA 92688, page 87, only 87 words total used from the whole book.

25 Baker, John Celebrate Recovery: Leader's Guide Updated, E-Book Published August 2009, Zondervan, only 208 words total used in this whole leader's guide from different spots stating the 8 principles.

Can you do a favor?

-   Please take a moment to write a review on this workbook on Amazon, Westbow, or Barnes and Noble. The time that you take to do this greatly appreciated.

Would you like to read other books by this author?

Exploring the Grace of God in Jonah

-   Tucked into the Old Testament is a book called Jonah. People do not usually think of God's grace in the Old Covenant, but it is there! Grace is defined as God's unmerited favor to us when we have not earned it. Jonah received God's grace in powerful ways. The way God offered it to him also can offer us fresh hope and encouragement too. Jonah was a man as you and I. The grace that he received is the grace we can experience too in our relationship with God.

What Covenant Do You Live By? The Answer May Surprise You

-   It all started with a statement. God expressed to me that I did not understand His grace and it affected my relationship with Him and other people. A journey began of which this book shares a little bit about in a Bible Study format. In this book you will learn the importance of living by the New Covenant instead of the Old Covenant as a born again Christian. This understanding brings a whole new way of seeing the Old Testament and New Testament through God's eyes. What can this Bible Study do for you? You will experience God's love in a greater way. You will experience God's grace more personally day to day. You will get more from reading your Bible. You will be able to help others who see God as out to get them. You will be more graceful with the people in your life.

Apollos and Me

- *"1 You then, my son, be strong in the grace that is in Christ Jesus. 2 And the things you have heard me say in the presence of many witnesses entrust to reliable people who will also be qualified to teach others"*, (2 Timothy 2:1-2). The Apostle Paul passed truths to Timothy and in turn asked him to do the same with others. This is a profound passage that applies to me as their things that God has taught me that I know are not to be kept to myself and are to be passed onto others. This book is about passing on the hopes of the baptism in the Holy Spirit, the gifts of the Holy Spirit, New Covenant, grace, and eternal security. Please do what I am doing and pass them onto others also!

God's Grace from Cover to Cover: Devotional 1

- I believe that God's grace is one topic that is very dear to His heart. It starts in the Old Testament and runs all the way through the New Testament if one has eyes to see it. He is a God of unmerited favor! It is His desire to show it to the unsaved and saved as part of the grand plan of dealing with mankind. Turn to the beginning of the Bible and you will find God creating the earth and its contents for mankind to enjoy. Adam and Eve never earned the animals that surrounded them or the scenic places to explore. Turn to the last pages of the Bible and you will find God providing a new heaven and earth for all the saved to enjoy. Not a single man or woman earned this privilege. It is a gift from God. In this book we will be looking at every reference of the word grace found in the Old Testament to 1 Corinthians 1 according to the New International Translation of the Bible. This format of looking at each one will let God's grace speak for itself and fill your heart with His unconditional love for you.

Would you like to learn more about the author?

https://cht4jesus.wixsite.com/charlesthompson
https://www.restoringhopehuntsville.com/